HOW TO WRITE YOUR BEST BUSINESS BOOK

HOW TO WRITE YOUR BEST BUSINESS BOOK

DR NICOLA RUSSELL JOHNSON

First published in Great Britain by Writing Dr
www.writingdr.com
Copyright © 2025 by Dr Nicola Russell Johnson & Peter Russell
All rights reserved.
No part of this book may be reproduced in any manner whatsoever without written permission except in the case of brief quotations embodied in critical articles and reviews.
First Printing, 2025

To Louise
You know why.

CONTENTS

FOREWORD	1
INTRODUCTION	4
INTRODUCTION MK.2	6
WHY HAVE A BOOK?	8
DO YOU HAVE THE AUTHORITY TO WRITE A BOOK?	15
YOUR AUDIENCE WANTS TO KNOW YOU	17
TARGET MARKET	20
WHAT'S YOUR BOOK ABOUT? WHAT'S GOING IN IT?	23
BOOK'S PURPOSE	28
PLAN – BOOK PLANNER	30
BOOK TITLE	34
COVER DESIGN	39
HOW LONG SHOULD YOUR BOOK BE?	41
KEY TAKEAWAYS	43
CALLS TO ACTION	46
RESEARCH	50

YOUR TIME USE IT	57
YOUR WRITING STYLE	67
ENGAGING YOUR READER	70
YOU KNOW YOUR GRAMMAR REALLY	80
EXISTING MATERIALS	93
CASE STUDIES	96
CLARITY	100
CHATGPT WRITE MY STORY!	104
WRITING COACH VS GHOSTWRITER VS AI	112
REVIEW: HOW MANY DRAFTS?	118
SELF-EDITING VS A FRIEND VS A PROFESSIONAL	122
EDITING - PROOFREADING - FORMATTING	127
FORMATTING WITH PETER	132
SOME REVIEW GUIDELINES	136
USE OF AI IN EDITING	141
TRADITIONAL PUBLISHING VS SELF-PUBLISHING VS HYBRI	145
HOW TO USE YOUR BOOK FOR LEADS	150
SELLING IT, PRICING IT, GIVING IT AWAY	153
BOOK DESCRIPTIONS AND KEY WORDS	157
CONCLUSION	159
ABOUT THE AUTHOR	162
CONNECT WITH US	164

FOREWORD

In 2017, I wrote a book about golf. Except it wasn't about golf, it was about improving your business. It was about taking what you do and making it a more viable source of income. It was about putting in the hard work and succeeding and about knowing your worth and shooting for the stars, or at least, shooting for the fairway with a single-digit handicap.

Sometimes in business, you have to choose whether to keep on with what you're doing, to send your golf ball flying safely, or if you're going to try to knock in the ball in fewer strokes, right over the hazards. It might be a tougher route, but if you nail it, you'll sink that hole in fewer shots.

What are you going to do?

Carry on like normal? Or give it a wazzer?

I'm a business coach, you might know me as the Fearless Business Coach, and business was going great when I decided in 2017 to give it a wazzer. I decided to write a book. It was called Take Your Shot, and it ended up being a bestseller.

I had a very good idea of the benefits of writing a book before I did it, but it surpassed every one of my expectations. It was, as it were, a hole-in-one.

Within the first year of its publication, I received 40 speaking gigs. And multiple invitations from notable podcasts. When I appeared on the Ali Abdaal Deep Dive podcast, I generated 3,000 leads. It was just a 2-hour interview, but it made all the difference.

And I got the interview – and the subsequent 3,000 inquiries – because I had a book.

I wasn't just Robin Waite, the Fearless Business Coach; I was Robin Waite, the bestselling author and Fearless Business Coach.

Every one of my clients has read Take Your Shot before they join the Fearless Crew. It made me stand out, it gave me the edge, and it gave me authority.

You can find everyone on the internet, on social media. It's a sea of voices all clamouring for your attention, and importantly, it's a sea of voices that are silenced the moment you shut your laptop or switch your phone off. A book continues to exist when the WiFi goes down. TikToks come and go, but a book stays in your clients' hands. Anyone can make media content, but a book builds credibility.

I'm standing here today with 6 books under my belt. I've done the work, I've swung the hard way, and I hit an Eagle, and I have to say, life and business look pretty damn good from here.

You have two choices. You can carry on as you are, or you can go the harder way, which could yield infinitely better results. You won't regret writing a book, but in a year's time, when your competition have their books written and published, you'll wish you'd swung harder. You'll wish that the trust and credibility that your competitors have were yours.

It's not easy. Maybe you haven't written anything of length since you were a student, but that shouldn't stop you. Getting a coach or even a ghostwriter can help you get your book done, and fast. They can help get your ideas on the page and keep you accountable. They can tell you what works and what doesn't.

You're the professional in your field, Dr Nicola Russell Johnson, and Peter Russell are the professionals in theirs. They have over 15 years of experience helping people to clarify their ideas and write them into books. If you're struggling or if you need an expert eye on it, they can help. After all, your book will show the world who you are and what you do, so you need to get it right.

I wholeheartedly encourage you all to write your business book. It feels pretty damn good and pretty damn busy to be a best seller. How To Write Your Best Business Book will show you the ropes, it'll give you the lay of the land; or in golfing terms, it'll give you a pre-round walkthrough, a bit of course reconnaissance.

Get rid of your doubts. Stop worrying about putting yourself out there. Don't fear what people might think of you. Be fearless. Write your book, it'll make a big difference to your business.

After all, [Insert Your Name Here] Bestselling Author has a nice ring to it, doesn't it!

And this could be you.

Robin Waite,

The Fearless Business Coach.

Author of Take Your Shot.

INTRODUCTION

Introductions. Who really reads them? Don't you just want to start learning how to write your best business book without having to sit through the whole Hullabaloo of an introduction?

Hullabaloo. I don't use that word enough. So, what have I got to say? What's so important you need to know it before you get reading this book?

Well, I suppose it's this: writing is easier and harder than you might think. Some people write too much, while others struggle to fill their word count. Some people enjoy it; some can't stand it.

Amongst all of these differences, there is one thing I want to stress.

Make your main aim this: try to write a book people will want to read.

That's more important than how many words you write or how many fancy words you use.

Never lose sight of your audience.

But first, read this book; it will show you exactly how to go about doing this.

Alright?

Okay, move along now, there's nothing to see here. It's just an introduction.

Go on.

Jog on, now.

INTRODUCTION MK.2

I have realised, while reviewing this book, that whilst my introduction is exactly how I want it, it doesn't help you, dear reader, understand how to write one. So, I'll tell you here how to do an introduction, but I want you to hold off actually writing it until you've completed your book. It should be the last thing you write.

Got it?

Right, your introduction needs to do the following things:

1. Address the reason for the book, often talking about the problems your book solves.
2. A promise that your book will help solve the problems.
3. Who you are, why you're awesome, and why you can tell people what to do.
4. A little outline of the book.

So, let's get cracking.

Want a book? Want a book but don't know where to start? Have you already written something, but it bores even you to tears? How

To Write Your Best Business Book will give you a dynamic look into the secrets to writing something people will actually want to read.

I'm Dr Nicola Russell Johnson, I have a PhD in Creative Writing, and I've spent the last 15 years helping people to write their books. Peter Russell is the interviewing, business, and publishing side of Writing Dr. He has top-notch interviewing skills from his time as a detective in the CID and is an accredited life coach. You'll be hearing from him from time to time in this book, whenever he has business, marketing, and publishing moments to teach you. Between us, we are Writing Dr. We can help you write the book, we can write it for you, and we can publish you.

Within these pages, we'll hold your hand through the beginning stages of writing your book, all the way to the end. Working on the Content, the Planning, the Writing, the Revising, and the Publishing.

I mean it, I'll hold your hand. So you better have washed it.

Right, that's enough to show you what to put in your introduction.

Now you can jog on.

WHY HAVE A BOOK?

The first time I had a machine gun pointed at my face, I was seventeen. The small aircraft I'd been in, flying over the Venezuelan rainforest, had been hijacked, and about ten of us holidaymakers were forced at gunpoint into a sort of shack that had been built by a makeshift runway strip. There was no food or water. It was hot. We had no idea how long we were going to be there or even if help was on its way at all.

And all I could think was, 'I could write the heck out of this in a short story one day.'

This is how I view life. This is the constant question in my mind: 'How will I narrate this after the event?'

And for a short while, this is how I want you to start viewing your life, because it could all be content for your book.

I'm making the assumption here that you want to write a book, and I think this is reasonable considering you're reading a guide called: 'HOW TO WRITE YOUR BEST BUSINESS BOOK'.

You might be the sort of person who reads guides for the fun of it and not because you're planning on carrying out the advice. Goodness knows that's how I now read Rick Stein's cookbooks after one of his recipes took me seven hours to make. Don't get me wrong, it was the best damn steak pie I've ever tasted, but I'll not be making it again. Seven hours!

So, you want a book?

Great!

You're in the right place, because I bloody love books.

However, first, I want to talk about why you should have a book. Don't skip this bit, because the reasoning here will help you gird your loins for the task of actually writing it. Any time you feel like stopping or taking a few weeks/months off writing, I'm going to suggest you come back to this chapter, to remind yourself why writing a book is a really good idea.

Before I continue, I'm just going to look up how one girds one's loins, because I can't imagine it's got anything to do with Kegel exercises.

Right, I'm back. Turns out girding one's loins isn't as exciting as pelvic floor exercises. It means to tie a belt or a girdle around your middle before a fight to stop your long clothes from getting in the way. So, if you're sitting down to write, may I suggest you ungird your loins and wear something comfortable, because you're going to be hunched over your notebook or computer for a while. The last thing you need is tight clothing. So let loose your loins and let's talk book.

There are a myriad of reasons why you should write a book. If you're running a successful business, if you're a coach of some kind, if you give talks or do podcasts, if you're aware of your online presence, a book is going to help you promote yourself further.

Think of it this way:

If you need to book an expert to talk at a conference and you have to choose between an expert versus an expert with a book, you're going to go with the expert with a book. A book will open doors for you in terms of speaking and media opportunities. Send your book to podcast hosts, media outlets, and event organisers. Your book will open up slots you otherwise would never have had access to.

It doesn't matter if you're looking for an expert on marketing, on promoting on social media, or on mapping the varicose veins of retired Philatelists in the Wapping area. You're going to choose the retired Philatelist from Wapping varicose vein mapper that's got the book out.

And that's what I want for you! I want them to always choose you!

So, you need a book.

Now, perhaps you work in a competitive field. Let's say there are a few of you doing what you do. A book will make you stand out from the crowd. It'll place you above your competitors. How do people choose whether to go with your company or with your rivals?

You need a book.

What if your competitor uses similar techniques to you, and they bring out a book first? You're going to miss out on clients and not because they're better than you, but because they put the effort in to write their book first. So, what should you do? Get writing ASAP or come along to Writing Dr to get your book written for you. Because if they have a book?

Then you need a book.

If you want to stamp your authority in your field. If you want everyone to know that you really know what you're talking about. You'll have noticed that AUTHOR is in authority! Gain yours by becoming an author.

You need a book.

If you want to promote more sales, if you want to reach more people, if you want to drive more traffic to your website?

You need a book.

You can use your book as your ultimate lead generation magnet. Who doesn't like something that's free? And when that free item is your book, your story, your wisdom, your ideal prospective clients are going to want to get their hands on it. They are going to download it, and then you can get them into your CRM (customer relations management system).

Not only are you generating leads, but leads that by the time they call you, or engage with you, have read about you, know you, know your products and services, and are ready to work with you or buy from you. We're talking incredibly warm leads here, being generated without you having to do any work on them, aside from writing your book!

You are no doubt incredibly good when it comes to social media, networking, SEO, building your client base, and ensuring that your ideal client can find you. However, where many services are not present, is on one of the biggest search engines out there, and a place where you will no doubt find yourself visiting for something at least once this week... Amazon.

Let's look at an accountant, for example, a potential client may well be on Amazon looking for a book on how to do their expenses, or self-assessment, or bookkeeping. If they are, then an accountant with a book on how self-employed people can do their own self-assessment has just expanded their pool of ideal clients that are searching for them, considerably.

And then, down the line, when the person who has bought this book (despite it being incredibly useful) decides they want a professional to do it instead because they can't do it themselves, or they don't have the time, where does this client go? Will they Google an unknown accountant or turn to the accountant whose book has been in their hands for the last 6-months. They're going to go to the person they have built a relationship with, that they trust, that they know has authority and credibility in their field, because they have been reading about them, they know them, and they have helped them.

This could be you!

You need a book!

It's better than a business card. Imagine the next time you're out networking, giving your ideal client your book rather than a business card. Because we all know a business card is going in the same pile as everyone else's. Your book, however, goes on their bookshelf, on their desk, by the side of their bed, or if it's really good, in the upstairs loo. Your ideal client could be reading about you 24/7. They could have access to you 24/7. And the whole time your book will be telling your story, building trust with your ideal client, and selling your products and/or services while you sleep.

You need a book!

It establishes your personal branding.

In today's crowded marketplace, your personal brand is more important than ever. Take a moment to think about how many competitors there are in your field, or think about the last time you required the services of, say, an accountant or solicitor, just how many options did you have to choose from? How can you set yourself apart from them? What is the ultimate tool you can use in terms of your personal branding?

A book!

Your book! Your book telling your story, showcasing your unique identity, describing your products and services, and the backstory behind them, demonstrating you as the thought leader in your field, the go-to person. And your book is going to outlast a brief conversation or a quick glance at a social media post.

And it will increase your potential customers' confidence in you and your service or product.

You need a book.

Seriously.

You need a book and you need it now.

And if you're confident in your field, it could be a lot quicker to write one than you think.

Think about how a book can help your ideal client, and indeed your current clients. If you offer courses or coaching services and you have a book, you can direct your clients to the relevant chapter, so they have a ready-made guide to follow. Isn't this exactly what educational institutes do? So, follow their lead! Your book can work alongside your course, products, or services.

So, start thinking the way I was thinking when I was seventeen and effectively in a hostage situation (we got out fine). Start collecting the moments of your life that define you, because you might need them later in the writing sections.

For now, I want you to think one thing.

You need a book.

Key Takeaways:

You're busy people and if, like me, when you read a book, you are looking to gain knowledge and take action, then key takeaways can be your friend. Or at least, they can be the guy that runs after you to let you know you've left your credit card in the ATM.

Throughout this book, at the end of each chapter, we'll list the key takeaways for you. This will aid you if you pick this book up for 5 minutes a day, or if you have read the book and want to return to a section to take action and start writing. You can revisit the key takeaways and get cracking.

- Be the expert in your field, gain the AUTHORity
- Generate more leads
- Expand your marketplace

- Convert more sales
- Your best business card
- Perfect personal branding tool
- Build trust with your ideal client
- Open speaking and media opportunities

We even have a handy 10-point checklist for you to download at writingdr.com/resources

DO YOU HAVE THE AUTHORITY TO WRITE A BOOK?

When I was 23 years old, I stepped into my first classroom of adult learners in Valencia after qualifying as a teacher of English as a foreign language. I was clearly the youngest person in the room, and I was objectively more scared than I had been in that Venezuelan shack.

The first thing one of those students asked me, within about five seconds of me being in the room, was, 'Do you always need the past participle when using the third conditional?'

I blanked out, said 'Yes!' then ran home frantically after the lesson to look it up in my enormous book of English grammar.

Luckily, I was right.

But something happened after I'd been a teacher for a while. I became comfortable saying, 'I'm not sure, let's look it up!' Because after a short time, I realised I was a bloody good teacher. I developed some excellent techniques to engage the class, and some great ways to help them retain what I was teaching.

I'll bet this is similar for a lot of you reading this book. You're good at what you do. You've developed some great techniques, you've got some brilliant success stories (keep a note of them, we'll be needing them later on), and you can really help people.

If you have doubts, that's okay. You can always run home and look up the usage of the past participle in the third conditional. Heck, research is an important part of any book. When I was studying under the late, great W. G. Sebald, he used to say that it didn't matter if you were writing fantasy where every plant and animal was a made-up creation, you still needed to do research.

And he was right.

He also used to think that that dog on the telly that could say 'sausages' was brilliant.

So, you know you can trust his advice. Because he was right about that dog, and he was right about the research.

If you're doing good work in your field, if you've got successes under your belt (whether it's girding your loins or not), if you've helped people, if you're comfortable talking about what you do and giving advice, then you have, you absolutely have the authority to write a book about it.

When I stepped into that classroom all those years ago, I was a qualified teacher. I absolutely had the authority to stand in front of those students and teach. I just needed to find that out for myself.

Working as you do, in your field, gives you the authority to write a book about it.

Trust me. I'm a doctor.

Key Takeaways:

- You are the expert, you have the authority
- Showcase your experience, qualifications, and success
- Research further for your book

YOUR AUDIENCE WANTS TO KNOW YOU

One afternoon, when I was teaching at a university in Japan, my classroom door was thrown open by a terrified-looking professor, who shouted that we all needed to get out and go home immediately. A typhoon was coming.

My students packed up and ran.

I was told the trains would stop running at any moment and that I had to get home fast.

I grabbed my bag, headed out of the university alongside swarms of people, pulled on my high heels, and speedwalked to the train station.

I'd never seen a typhoon before, but already the winds had picked up and the rain was starting to fall.

The thing is, I was also hungry. And at the station before my stop, there was an incredible fast-food restaurant that did the most wonderful chilli burger I'd ever tasted in my life.

So instead of going straight home, I got off the train one stop early and battled my way through what was now a full-blown typhoon. There were five steps leading up to the front door of the fast-food place, and I vividly remember clinging onto the railing, pulling myself up in my high heels as the wind and the rain did their best to literally sweep me away into the unknown.

When I struggled my way through the doors, the staff, who were hunkering down in the restaurant, were looking at me in horror. Then they made me a burger. The manager said it was a great endorsement of their food. And you know what?

It was worth it.

That's who you're dealing with when you come to me. You're dealing with a woman who would battle a category three typhoon in high heels for a damn chilli burger.

And your audience wants to know who they're dealing with when they read your book, too.

They really want to know about you.

Now, personal branding is important nowadays, and it's particularly vital when writing your book. Before people will trust you, they need to know who you are.

I'm not saying you should tell everyone your mother's maiden name, the street you grew up on, and your NHS number. I'm not saying you should've kept a chart of your bowel movements during the 2022 World Cup and how they were affected by the number of red cards given and the type of beer you drank each match. But you should let people know a bit about you. If people can get a real feel for you, it can really sway their decisions to come to you as a client.

Most people also find it's not always easy to read long documents that don't have a human element to them. I always say that you could put the meaning of life on page 42, but if your book is too dry, nobody will get past page 28 to find it out.

I'll talk more about using your life to engage the reader in the writing section, but right now, it's important for you to know that inserting yourself into your book will inspire more confidence in you from your clients. They may feel like they get to know you. They may feel a kinship to you that will inspire them to become loyal to your brand rather than an unknown, cheaper company that doesn't have a book or much personal branding.

So, when people are choosing a company to work with, they'll already like you, trust you, and have a good idea of how you work before they've even had their first meeting with you. Professionalism is great but so is being human.

Be authentic. Be you. Unless you're a horrible person, then be David Attenborough; he's supposed to be lovely.

I want you to shine. And your book is your time and your place. You control the narrative.

I dare say, with everyone posting on social media nowadays, you'll already have an idea of how you come across and what your personal branding is, so I think you can do this. And if you can't? If it all gets a bit too much or if you don't have the time? Come and speak to us at Writing Dr. We have an accredited coach to pull the ideas out of your head and a doctor of Creative Writing (moi) to slam those ideas down onto the page, using your voice, your personality, and your style. Or David Attenborough's style, you know, if you happen to be despicable and need to hide it...

Key Takeaways:

- Your ideal client wants to know you
- Build a relationship with your reader
- Be you
- Use your book as your ultimate personal branding tool
- Can't do it? Don't have the time? Book a call with Nicola and Peter (you know us) writingdr.com/book-a-call

TARGET MARKET

It's not just vital to know what you're writing about; it's also important to know who you're writing for.

At this stage in your career, you'll probably have a clear idea of who your target market is. So, think about the kind of language that works best with them. Think of your social media posts that have gained the most traction. Think of talks you've given where you can tell your audience is really engaged. Think of the last time you spoke to a client where you knew you were talking their language.

And address those pain points. What problems do your clients have? How badly do they want them fixed?

All of these techniques are the same ones I want you to employ in your writing. Just because you're writing a book rather than a social media post doesn't mean you suddenly have to start writing highbrow literature. That is, unless your target market loves highbrow literature, in which case, have at it.

Today's successful business books often take into account that, as a species, the length of our attention spans has reduced significantly. Is this also true for your target market? If so, split your writing into shorter paragraphs, use lots of subheadings, and get to the point.

There are also differences in the way you should write, depending on your audience. Is your target market heavily into tech? Into memes? Into contemporary culture? Are they older? Younger? All of these can factor into how you write. As a very simple example, I write differently for an American audience than I do for a British audience. In fact, a blog I ghostwrote for an American client ended up winning a big award. That same blog would probably not have even been shortlisted in the UK because the taste between the two markets is just different. And it's more than just spelling differences; it's differences in culture, philosophy, and outlook.

The brilliant news for you here is that you undoubtedly know your target market better than anyone. So, dig deep, my friend. Make yourself a little profile board of who your target market is and what they want. Make it look like a detective's whiteboard on a criminal investigation show.

And then?

Well, you always give the customer what they want, right? Unless your customer is trying to buy three hatchets, a roll of tarp, and four bottles of strong bleach. If that's the case, don't give the customer what they want, tell them to step to one side, and make a call to the police.

All of this is to say, there's no point writing like People's Friend if you want Gen X to read it. If you write like Women's Weekly when your target market is academics, it's not going to go down well. Sorry, Vera from Chipping Sodbury, your back page tip about using clothes pegs to seal half-eaten bags of crisps came as a revelation to many, I'm sure.

Now, if you work in a field where you do not come across your clients face-to-face or eyes to social media, then do a little research. Find out who your clients are, what interests they have. See if you can find them on social media and get a feel for how they talk and how they like to be talked to. Read other books in your field. Look at what has been successful and what hasn't, and make a note of it.

Because when it comes right down to it, you're writing this book for them. So, gear it towards them.

Key Takeaways:

- Who is your book for?
- How are they going to use it?
- What do you want them to do when they read it?

And for you...it may well be useful to buy our Book Planner at this point to help guide you 'HOW TO WRITE YOUR BEST BUSINESS BOOK – BOOK PLANNER'.

Or jump on a call with Nicola and Peter to discuss who your book is for before you start writing.

writingdr.com/book-a-call

WHAT'S YOUR BOOK ABOUT? WHAT'S GOING IN IT?

This might seem quite obvious, but you'd be surprised how many writers lose their way a bit.

When writing a non-fiction book, you have an advantage over the fiction writer. People pick up fiction books because they like the author, they like the cover, they like the genre, it's on offer, or they have 15 minutes before their flight and only have time to grab what's nearest the till. Maybe it's a free eBook. Maybe it's a recommendation.

However, people pick up a non-fiction business/coaching book for one main reason: They specifically want to learn what the book promises to teach.

Very few people would take a suitcase of books on marketing and social media optimisation on their holiday to Marbella. That's what trashy thrillers are for. Many people, however, see a gap in their knowledge or abilities and buy a book to teach them how to do and be better.

This is a great power that you possess. It's a huge advantage you have over the fiction readers. Your readers are hungry for the knowledge and skills stored away in your book.

Now I've talked a little bit already about stuffing a few of your life experiences into your book, and I really do recommend doing this, but do take care. I have read books that start with a 70-odd page autobiography before they even begin imparting the, hopefully, golden information and the techniques to improve your business. What's worse is sometimes the author doesn't really come out of it looking like a particularly nice or trustworthy person. I'll be willing to bet a lot of readers even skip or skim the whole first half of many books that do this.

I don't want this to be you.

Instead, think about imparting little bits of gold in each chapter. Keep your life story to fewer than 70 pages and make it interesting and relevant. Use it to get your readers on your side. Because once your readers' attention starts to waver, you could lose them for good. They'll start skipping chapters that may be vital to the process you're teaching. And once they've lost interest, it's incredibly hard to bring them back into your book without doing some sort of flashy trick like shouting:

'YOU'RE NEVER GOING TO BELIEVE WHAT MY NEXT TIP IS!'

Or some other literary equivalent to clickbait.

After saying this, clickbait-style subheadings can work brilliantly. No shame in it.

YOU'RE NEVER GOING TO BELIEVE THIS TIP TO DRIVE MORE CUSTOMERS INTO YOUR CRM!

Here's something else that can work well for you in a book. Add in your website, your social media handles, and your QR codes. You can guide readers to your website to see pictures of what you're talking about in your book. If you have a nifty chart? Think about getting your readers to go online to see it. Get them to email you to find out extra tips or secrets. Think of it as being more interactive than a standard book and really use it to drive traffic to your website and business. Prey on your readers' curiosity. There are so many possibilities out there. I recently read a great business book where the author told us that he looked like a potato. I was so curious, I followed the link to see for myself. And BAM, I'm on his website.

Make sure you include calls to action. Plenty of them. Not so many that you lose your reader, keep them relevant to what you're talking about, and make sure they go where you want them to go.

And if this doesn't really make sense to you, why not book a call with us at Writing Dr, and we can talk through it with you and how you can personalise these ideas in your particular book.

writingdr.com/book-a-call

So, in short, do include anecdotes from your life and business. Don't waffle on too long; your readers want to learn. If they wanted a straight autobiography, they'd have bought one of David Attenborough's.

Do make sure to include teachable moments throughout. Don't get sidetracked into talking about other business things. And finally, do add in calls to action and steer people towards your website and your CRM. Use your business book as a tool for you as much as a tool for your reader. Let's make it a two-way street!

Key takeaways:

- What is going in your book?
- What do you want to tell your ideal client?
- Find the right balance between telling them about you and it becoming an autobiography
- Keep your reader engaged
- Add value for your reader
- Where do you want your reader to go when they read your book?

We'd love for you to come visit us at writingdr.com

Then take a look through our resources, or book a call with Nicola and Peter.

And come join us on our social media channels:

Linked In
www.linkedin.com/in/peter-russell-writing-coach-and-publisher-280149208/
www.linkedin.com/in/dr-nicola-russell-johnson-711619350/
Facebook
www.facebook.com/peter.russell.927
www.facebook.com/nicola.russelljohnson
Tik Tok
www.tiktok.com/@writingdr.com
Instagram
www.instagram.com/writingdrs/
You Tube
www.youtube.com/@Writing_Dr

BOOK'S PURPOSE

This chapter serves as a summary, but it's useful for consolidating your ideas. It's a good idea to think about what your book's main purpose is before you write it. This will help pull your ideas into focus. Business books have several different purposes:

1. You want to help people.
2. You want to advertise your services.
3. You want to establish your intellectual property.
4. You want authority in your field.
5. You want to drive traffic to your website.
6. You want publicity.
7. You want to use it for marketing purposes.
8. You want to use it as a lead generator.

A well-written book can do all these things. Easily. And they're all great reasons to write a book in terms of your book's legacy. Once it's released into the wild, it'll be connecting you with people even as you sleep. You'll forever be known as the guru of your field.

Whether you write the book or get your book ghostwritten, it's just a really good idea to get it done and out there. If you're serious about what you do, if you're good at what you do, if you want more clients to find you, if you want to be booked for more speaking roles, get a book.

Don't dither about it. The chances are your competition isn't dithering. Get one started today.

PLAN – BOOK PLANNER

To plan or not to plan, that is the question.
I'm going to stop myself here. There's no question about it. Plan it.

There are a few magic beings who can write books without planning them. They are the anomaly. There is something off about them. Every so often, a famous author will go on the record saying that they never plan their books. That they write by the seat of their pants. That they start writing and see where it takes them.

Don't listen to them.

Plan it.

Planning your book before you write it is absolutely vital. I know a writer who had to ditch 85,000 words because they hadn't planned in advance and had written themselves into a corner. I will never forget the look on their face. And I imagine since then, they've planned before writing ever since.

I'm a huge planner. Often, I plan for longer than I write. I spent eleven years researching and planning my PhD before writing it. When you plan, wonderful things happen. You can include themes and tropes. You can pick out patterns. You can create cliffhangers at the end of chapters. Your book can be a meaningful, exciting, and unwavering journey.

If you don't plan, terrible things may befall you. You might lose track of where you're going. You could lose focus. You could forget important things. You could end up ditching 85,000 words. You may accidentally begin a nuclear war in Cuba, you might step on Lego, or worst of all: You might get writer's block.

And writer's block is bloody awful.

Now, I've been writing for other people for 15 years. I know the ins and outs of writer's block, but if this is your first book, you might not appreciate how bad it is.

I once had a flight delayed for 27 hours while suffering from cystitis at Heathrow Airport.

Writer's block is worse than that.

I once ate leftover cream cake that had sat on the kitchen counter overnight in the desert in Mexico. I didn't leave the bathroom for three days.

Writer's block is worse than that.

I once had a chunk of my eyeball gouged out.

No. No, now that one was worse than writer's block. Thank God for numbing eye drops and strong painkillers.

You get the gist of it, though.

Once writer's block hits, you can be left with thousands of words in limbo. And I'm not talking about the fun kind of limbo where you drink tequila and try to walk bent over backwards under a stick. I'm talking about that lost in the middle of nowhere limbo. Because without the end, the beginning and middle may as well not have even been written. And if it's your first time with writer's block, you may find yourself giving up altogether.

However, if you've planned your book in advance, you'll help stave off the ominous gloom of writer's block. You'll know exactly what you need to write, and while the words may not be the best, you can always go back and edit them at the end.

If you have a good, clear, detailed plan, you can effectively write yourself out of writer's block.

It's also worth keeping in mind that if you do end up experiencing writer's block and are really struggling, sometimes talking it out with someone can help you through it. Plus, you can come to us here at Writing Dr and we can talk you through it. Or, if you need it, finish writing it for you.

DO NOT LET WRITER'S BLOCK STOP YOU FROM GETTING A BOOK DONE!

Don't let it win!

Some people sit on half-finished books for years!

What a flipping shame that would be.

If this is you, come on over to writingdr.com, and in a matter of months, you could be signing your books after talks, people could be holding them in their hands, instead of it being in some dusty computer file that you never open.

So, plan it. Plan every chapter. Plan every anecdote. Plan it in as much detail as you can. Plan it like you're a Bond villain aiming to take down Western civilisation.

I want you to view each chapter as if it were a tiny book in itself. Have a beginning, middle, and an end. Often, business books like to have a little recap at the end, distilling everything down to a few sentences. This is fine. Maybe you could also give your readers a reason to keep reading by hinting at what is to come next, too.

When you plan each chapter like this, it can really help with your mindset. Because instead of looking at the prospect of writing 30,000 words, you can just focus on each 1,000-word chapter. Taking it one step at a time.

Easy!

Key Takeaways:

- Planning is essential
- Plan before you do anything else
- What is your book's purpose
- What is going into the book
- Plan out your chapters
- Plan what is going in each chapter
- PLAN!!!

We have a free book planner on our website writingdr.com/resources for you to use, or our Book Planner is available on Amazon, 'HOW TO WRITE YOUR BEST BUSINESS BOOK – BOOK PLANNER'.

BOOK TITLE

Book titles are desperately important. Every so often you'll see flashes of absolute genius when it comes to titles. 'Tart of Darkness', 'Everything I Know About Women I learned From My Tractor', and 'Shaving Ryan's Privates' come instantly to mind.

With business and coaching books, you can choose to go with something that tells the reader exactly what it does, for example:

'The 7 Habits of Highly Effective People'
'Getting Things Done: The Art of Stress-Free Productivity'
'Think and Grow Rich'
Or you can go with something a little more fun:
'Life's Work: Confessions of an Unbalanced Mom'
'If You Can't Live Without Me, Why Aren't You Dead Yet?'
'How To Raise Your IQ By Eating Gifted Children'
Or you can go with something that can provoke some sort of emotion, whether it's positive or negative:
'Bootstrap Your Life'
'Chip War'
'The E-Myth Revisited: Why Most Small Businesses Don't Work and What to Do About It'
All of these are good ways to title your book.

Bad ways to title your book are by being vague, dull, or confusing. Now I'm not about to shame any writers' book titles here, but I would like to add this utterly glorious title to my list. I think it goes perfectly under funny and confusing:

'The Jewish Japanese Sex and Cookbook and How to Raise Wolves'

You might get your title before even starting to write your book. If so, you're living the dream! Other times, the title might come halfway through, maybe it could even come from a phrase you find yourself using over and over again. Or, and this is what happens most of the time, you might finish your book with no clue what to call it. In fact, there's a special kind of writer's block that can happen simply over choosing your title. Every writer has experienced it. Every writer has also experienced coming up with a title they adore, only to be told by their editor that they need to change it.

So, what do you do if you have title writing writer's block?

Can you reduce the main goal of your book to one sentence? You could go with that.

Can you think of an idiom or an historical quote you can work with?

Sometimes, lovely, long, slightly weird titles work well.

Write all of them down, everything you can think of. Speak to friends and colleagues, see what they say. This is the one time Jim next door might actually be of some use!

CONSIDER EVERYTHING

Write down even the bad ones. Sometimes we can learn from seeing what not to do and figuring out why that is (and I'll come back to this later because it's an important writing point to me).

Think about what titles are successful in other formats, social media and videos, for example.

DON'T LOSE SIGHT OF YOUR CLIENTS

It's also a good idea to think first of what you think your ideal client would search for when looking for a book. Are they likely to type in 'hedge maintenance for complete utter imbeciles'? If they are, you might have found your title. Don't forget SEO words can be your friend here, so it's worth making a list of them and considering using them in your title. Your list won't go to waste, as you'll need it later when you sell your book on Amazon, so really go for it.

DON'T FREAK OUT

But also, don't get too hung up on this. Don't stress out to the point of freezing up. Titles are important, and they can make the difference between someone selecting your book over a competitor's, but you also have an advantage over the fiction writer. People will buy your book because they want to learn the specific knowledge you're imparting within it. This means you could call it:

'Observing the behaviour of eczema on the legs of quantity surveyors during the tax season.'

And people who want to know about it will buy it.

If you need help with titles, you can come and chat it over with us at Writing Dr.

CHAPTER TITLES

Now, a business book will also often name its chapters. There's less pressure here to come up with something genius. Most people just want to know what the chapter is about. Especially people who may want to dip in and out of your book. My advice here is to be nice and clear. Even if you're being funny (which is always a good idea), be clear about what is going to be in that chapter. For example:

HOW TO KEEP FRIENDS AFTER INFECTING THEM WITH PARASITES, WORMING YOUR WAY BACK INTO THEIR GOOD BOOKS

SUBHEADINGS

On top of giving your chapters titles, non-fiction, particularly business and coaching books, have the rather splendid option of using subheadings. Subheadings are a great way to break your book down into nice digestible chunks. And the easier it is to digest, the easier it is to hold your reader's attention.

You might also personally find it easier to write this way, as it could feel a little more like writing separate social media posts than staring into the void of 30,000+ unwritten words. Fiction writers don't really get to use subheadings; this is an advantage only available to you lot. So, snap it up and utilise it!

Key Takeaways:
- Tells the reader what it does
- What would resonate with your ideal client?
- A title which aligns with your branding, products, services, and values
- Grabs people's attention (crowded marketplace out there)
- Think keyword search
- List multiple potential titles before settling on one
- Chapter titles
- Use your chapter titles to help break up writing your book
- Align to your social media posts/blogs/services

COVER DESIGN

Alright, are you going to say it, or shall I?
You shouldn't judge a book by its cover. But we all do it!

This means you want to impress your readers right from the get-go. You need a professional and dynamic front cover.

It's a good idea, once more, to do some research. Check out what's out there already. Which covers work? Which aren't so effective?

Next, think about your target audience. What sort of thing would they go for?

Finally, think about all the other people you need to attract: podcast hosts, event organisers, and potential partners.

What are you going to do to make your book stand out? How can you make it leap off the screen to someone scrolling down Amazon?

It's also worth keeping in mind your branding. Can you make a cover in keeping with your personal branding? Try using your brand colours or logo so that it's an extension of your company.

Don't go for anything that looks less than professional, unless you're doing it for a particular reason.

Sometimes people like simplicity, so, try not to have a cluttered front cover. Think clean lines and bold, easy-to-decipher images. Remember to set the tone of your book with your cover. It's the first impression so, make it a lasting one.

Mock up a bunch of covers and get friends, colleagues, and Jim down the road to whittle them down to just a few. Then you can tease the release of your book by getting your social media followers to vote on their favourite. You'll get feedback while doing a nice bit of marketing. Two birds, one cup! I mean stone!

Key Takeaways:

- First impressions count
- Attract your target audience
- Stand out in a crowd
- Enhance your brand
- Align with your branding
- Instant credibility
- Simplicity
- Professional
- Sets the tone

HOW LONG SHOULD YOUR BOOK BE?

Well, this can vary. I'd say it's best to write a minimum of 30,000 words. If you need to make it longer, then go for it. As long as you are writing engaging and helpful advice, you can make it as long as you like. However, if you've got 20,000 excess words of waffle, self-indulgence, or repetition, then it's best to cut it. Every so often, I come across a 60,000-word business book that would've been better and more impactful had it only 30,000 words. Books like this are in danger of losing their readers' interest, attention, and, to an extent, respect.

Your book should be focused, not meandering. Remember, the primary reason people are reading your books is to learn something, not to enjoy three-page descriptions of Dorset in April. We've got Thomas Hardy for that.

A general rule is that your book should be approximately 30,000 words, with each chapter ranging from 1,000 to 1,500 words in length.

However, I hate rules, and if you come up with a way to make it work, go ahead and do things differently!

You can make your chapters longer, for example, by breaking them up into nifty little subheadings.

You can make your book longer by being engaging and distributing flashes of genius.

I've seen books where every chapter is one page long. It made for snappy reading.

If you're writing a book to establish yourself in your field and drive traffic to your website and CRM, though, I recommend keeping it not too long. Make it as informative, affirmative, and entertaining as possible, while giving your readers good reasons to work with you.

Key Takeaways:

- Most business books are 30,000 words
- Is what you're writing relevant and useful to the reader?
- Write to keep your reader engaged
- Purposeful – you want people coming into your CRM, working with you, buying from you

KEY TAKEAWAYS

You're busy people, and the chances are, when you read a book, you are looking to gain knowledge and take action.

Throughout this book, you will have noticed that at the end of each chapter, we list the key takeaways for you. This will aid you if you pick this book up for 5 minutes a day, or if you have read the book and want to return to a section to take action and start writing. You can visit this section, get your pen out, and start writing your book.

Key Takeaways can really benefit skim readers, and they can also serve to remind your reader that you're giving good advice and they're getting their money's worth when they buy your book. It's quite nice to boil each chapter down to its bare bones and key elements. It can also really help you in the planning stages of your book in order to keep your chapters focused.

Whenever Peter attends a conference, event, or meeting, he looks for the key takeaways, the thing that he could take back to his teams and share in a briefing, the thing that could make a difference to his people, the things that could make work lives easier, increase performance, increase leads, and/or sales. He approaches books in much the same way. And so, when Peter reads a non-fiction/how-to/business book, even for pleasure, he will be looking for the items within it that can help him right now, something that he can read and put into practice.

With many books or seminars, he'd find himself making notes, countless notes, but when he comes across a book that has key takeaways and actions summarised, he breathes a sigh of relief. And while yes, he does read the book or the chapter, he knows that he can easily find the part of the book where the actions are that he needs to take.

When teaching and instructing people, going over your main points can be useful.

As teachers, we were told to put clear goals for the lesson plans and summarise the learning points, go over what the students had learnt, and ensure that when they left the classroom, they were fully aware of what they'd learnt and how to use it. You'll notice that educational books will all have these. So, use them in your books, your reader, your ideal client will really thank you for them.

If this book right now were to give you three key takeaways so far, it'd be:

1. Plan your book.
2. Write for your audience.
3. Never leave cream cake out of the fridge overnight in the desert in Mexico.

Seriously, I exited that bathroom two sizes smaller than I went in.

Business books can also utilise all sorts of bullet points, text boxes, and standalone comments. All of these can help solidify your main points and can help break up any heavy reading that your audience may struggle with.

Key Takeaways:

- Use key takeaways!!!
- Use them to summarise the key points of the chapter
- Use them to help your reader take immediate actions
- Use them to help your reader understand/cement what they have just learnt from you

CALLS TO ACTION

If you are using your book to drive traffic to your website/company, then don't be afraid to use calls to action within your book. Clever business books use varying techniques, and all can be wildly successful.

Think about directing your readers to your website to see photos or pictures or diagrams that are particularly interesting or useful. Most of us have our phone close to hand, or may even be reading your book on one, and will often sneak a look at a recommended picture.

You can direct your readers to your website to take a quiz to better understand their personality or issues. Here at Writing Dr, we have a small quiz to show how your personality type could impact the way you write, with dos and don'ts and recommendations. Try it out now: writingdr.com/resources

People like to be interactive, and a lot of business books nowadays don't just state website addresses; they contain QR codes to make it even easier.

Make your book work for you! It can be a great marketing tool. You could even tell readers that they can reach a special extra chapter by following a QR code. Before you know it, they're on your website. They know you. They know what you do. And they like you, because they've read your book. Now they're coming to your website for extras.

It's a bit like theme park roller coasters that exit into a gift shop. They do it because it works. Plus, I'm a sucker for a fridge magnet.

Key Takeaways:

- What are your calls to action?

- Where do you want your reader to go?
- What action do you want them to take? Book a call? Buy your product? Join a group?
- Make it easy for your reader to go to them
- Use them sparingly. Every chapter can get a bit repetitive
- Make them relevant

What do we want you to do?

Well ultimately, we just really want you to write your book. However, if you need help, then we'd love you to come to us. So, ours works like this:

You start following us. If you have bought this in a shop, or online, we don't know you yet, but you're getting to know us. If you've got this book after one of our talks or workshops, then you'll have a pretty good idea of who we are. We'd like you to make the connection and come and join us on our social media channels and let us know what you think of this book.

Linked In
www.linkedin.com/in/peter-russell-writing-coach-and-publisher-280149208/
www.linkedin.com/in/dr-nicola-russell-johnson-711619350/
Facebook
www.facebook.com/peter.russell.927
www.facebook.com/nicola.russelljohnson
Tik Tok
www.tiktok.com/@writingdr.com
Instagram
www.instagram.com/writingdrs/
You Tube
www.youtube.com/@Writing_Dr

Then we'd love for you to come visit us at writingdr.com, check out our resources, download some, get your details entered into our CRM, so we know who you are and can keep you up to date with our products, services, and some motivation to get your book written.

Then book a call with Nicola and Peter and use us to get your book written and published. writingdr.com/book-a-call

And finally, use your book to do exactly this for you and your business, and watch the leads and sales grow!

So, through our book, where relevant, you will see our links, and our calls to action. And we'll see you on a call soon.

RESEARCH

Now, I've already mentioned W. G. Sebald and his opinions on researching and dogs that say 'sausages'. I've also mentioned my own love of research, although I have to say, I quite like dogs that say 'sausages' too.

This part is the second most exciting part of writing a book. Research!

You may be a leading expert in your field. I still want you to do research.

Don't know where to start? Well, I'll tell you.

First things first, go and take a look at as many other books in your field as you can. (Get them from your local library if you don't want to increase your competitors' sales.)

It's important to see what is out there already.

Make a note of what these books do well and where they go wrong. And I really want you to think hard about this. Often, when I talk to business people about business books, I find that they don't always critically understand when a book is bad. They're so focussed on whether it has anything useful to teach that they often don't pinpoint why they only read half of it, or why they only skim read it, or why they just picked out a few chapters.

I think this is because people who don't come from an academic, literary background are reluctant to think it's the book's fault if they don't manage to read it all the way through.

They think it's their fault!

Maybe they think they're not great readers, or their attention span is too short. I think they honestly believe that other people, who are better with books, are reading these same books cover to cover and loving them.

Listen to me carefully here.

In this day and age, any contemporary book, especially non-fiction, business, and coaching books, should be easy and enjoyable to read.

It's okay if you struggle to read Joseph Conrad's Heart of Darkness; it's a heavy subject written in a different age. I read it in four hours, and while it was amazing, dear Lordi, the horror, the horror.

If you are reading a book from your field, you are, amongst others, the correct audience to be reading that book.

And if you can't get through it?

If you find yourself skimming and skipping bits?

It doesn't mean there's something wrong with you. It means there's something wrong with the book.

It's a bit of an 'it's not you, it's me' situation, except this time, 'it's not you, it's the book'.

I want you to have confidence when you read a book that it might not be any good, and you are in a position to recognise that if you find yourself skipping bits. I've dedicated my life to the written word, so if I'm reading a book and my eyes start to glaze over and I begin contemplating cleaning out the cupboard under the stairs, do you think I assume other people might be enjoying it? That maybe I have a concentration issue?

No!

If I'm thinking of cleaning out the cupboard under the stairs, it means the book sucks.

And it probably sucks harder than the vacuum cleaner I keep in the cupboard under the stairs, which doesn't seem to be able to pick up a damn thing right now. I might need to clean out the filter.

So, read as many books as you can get your mitts on and feel confident in your ability to judge them. Here are some examples of things to look out for. I'll start with the positives and then the negatives.

How do you know a business book is well written?

1. You enjoy reading it.
2. You find yourself wanting to read just one more chapter.
3. You'd rather read it than play Angry Candy Crush Birds.
4. It has clear and useful information.
5. It makes you feel confident in the writer's authority.
6. It incentivises you; it pumps you up, it makes you feel like you can do it.

The negatives are the opposites of the above.

1. You find yourself skim-reading.
2. You skip pages.
3. You start thinking of other things while reading.
4. You come away unsure if you've learnt anything.
5. The advice feels janky.
6. It's filled with clichés.

When you read other business books, I want you to take note of what they did well so that you can utilise the same techniques. Don't write down what you think you should like; write down what you actually like about those books.

You might love mnemonics, you might hate them, for example. Make a note of this. If a Venn diagram doesn't explain things any clearer than the text, make a note. If you prefer bar charts, make a note.

It's important to know who has come before you, before you write.

The next part of researching your business/coaching books is to look at the social, historical, and psychological impact of your field and what you're about to write about. You may not actually include Carl Jung in your books, but it's important to know his theories on your field.

This is the time to voraciously digest everything you can in your field. You're not going to include it all, but it will all be a seriously strong foundation on which to write your books.

It's a good time here to talk about how many non-fiction books like to start their chapters with an inspirational quote. Please, for the love of Sam Ryder, research the person you are quoting. I have worked on many books that accidentally utilise inspirational quotes from absolutely despicable people. I've literally seen go get 'em quotes by people who are currently in prison for running a Ponzi scheme! I don't care if a neo-Nazi said something that really made you want to be a better quantity surveyor, don't use their quote. You know that saying, 'What do you get if you sit down at a table with 10 nazis? 11 nazis.' Well, that also goes for the kinds of people you choose to quote. So, take care, and look into the people you're quoting.

To highlight great quotes from despicable people, I thought I'd add some in. In fact, I dallied a little with the idea of starting all of the chapters hereon with an amazing quote from an awful person. Then I realised I really need to be saved from myself sometimes.

I am however, going to stuff some in here, because wow.

'Words build bridges into unexplored regions.'

Adolf Hitler

'I believe in one thing only, the power of human will.'

Joseph Stalin

'In order for you to succeed, your desire for success should be greater than your fear of failure.'

Bill Cosby

'Women hold up half of the sky.'

Mao Zedong

'Society's needs come before the individual's needs.'

Hitler again.

'Faith moves mountains, but only knowledge moves them to the right place.'

Joseph Goebbels

'Art is the most endearing investment.'

Yep, it's Hitler again.

'Can you tell what it is yet?'

Rolf Harris

When I ghostwrite for people, I study everything I can get hold of. I even study the landscape in which the book is set. The flora, the fauna, the politics, the culture. I unfortunately forget most of it by the time I start writing my next book, but for a glorious moment, I'm an expert in whatever field it is I'm looking into. Not just of the field, but of the writing techniques people use to write about the field.

For short periods of my life, I've been an expert on camels, Cleveland psychiatric facilities, DIY large water filters, cumulus cloud formation, the ancient art of New Mexico, and translation software. That's just naming a few. If I'm writing about it, I'm studying it.

Research is glorious. You'll find it inspiring, helping you with both the planning and the writing of your book, and it's validating to have proper research behind your ideas. You'll be even more confident when you write.

You may have lived a very full and varied life. If so, brilliant. I absolutely want to hear about it, and I'll be talking about that later on in the book. But your own experiences aren't enough on their own. Research your subject first.

Part of your research should also be on the writing style of your peers. Does it work? Does it fall flat? What techniques worked well? Which bits did you like? You can utilise all of these things in your own book. You can also learn from what they did wrong. If something was written in a particularly dull way, spot it, and don't do it yourself!

So, learn to love research! Also, keep a notebook of all the research you do. If you like a concept or a sentence, jot it down with the book, page number, author, and year of the book's publication. Keep it all in the same book so you don't lose it. If and when you use one of these quotes or references, you can use it, reference it, and stick it in your bibliography without having to dig the book up again.

Right, that's it! Except, did you know camels can drink saltwater? They process the salt from the water, keep the water in, and spit the salt out! Marvelous creatures! Marvelous, great, lumbering, smelly creatures!

Key Takeaways:

- Research is essential, even with you being an expert, make sure it is right!

- Competitor analysis, what is out there? What do you like/dislike about their books?
- Make your book readable. How many books do you struggle to read/finish?
- What writing is out there on your topic already?
- How will yours be better/different?
- Do you agree/disagree with other leading figures in your field?
- Research who you're quoting, check that you want to be linked to them!

YOUR TIME USE IT

Your time is precious, so make it count. The last thing you need to be doing when you find the time to write, is to stall, get struck with writer's block, or find yourself scrolling FB or playing that game that you love/hate playing.

Here are some top tips that work for me, take a look through and work out which ones are a good fit for you and then write!

MAKE EVERY MINUTE COUNT

Before you sit down to write, think about what you are going to do and achieve in that time, then make every minute count. If you find yourself stuck on something, is there another writing task that you could be doing, and come back to that one when unstuck later, or after a coaching session to unstick yourself on it.

HOW MUCH TIME DO YOU HAVE TO WRITE?

Work out what a realistic time is that you can set aside a week, consider this as a formula as to how long it will take you to write your book.

Your book is likely to end up being about 30,000 words. If you target 500 words a day and write every day, you're looking at having that book written in 60 days! Easy!

To get 500 words a day, you are likely to need half an hour.

However, what works best for you? Is half an hour a day best for you, or an hour every other day? Or wait until the weekend, or hump day and devote 3 ½ hours to it. People often find that when they are in the zone, it is best to crack on, so doing it all in one chunk may work best. Alternatively, 30 minutes a day may fit perfectly into your routine, and it beats scrolling FB or playing that game that you love/hate playing.

Lots of businesses have been looking at four-day weeks, and employees have been using their fifth day for CPD, courses, or volunteering. Why not think about using your fifth day to write your book?

30 minutes a day/3 ½ hours a week, what would work best for you?

BEST TIME OF DAY TO THINK/WRITE

When are you at your most creative? Many people find that first thing in the morning is when they are most able to focus on tasks, get stuff written, and be at their most creative. Would getting up half an hour earlier each morning work for you?

Or are you a night owl, finding that creative spark and a moment to yourself once the kids have gone to bed and you've scrolled through the TV channels 5 times and found nothing to watch.

And I'm not advocating a drink here, but Hemingway is famously misquoted as saying "Write drunk, edit sober". If a glass of red allows the pen to flow easier, or you gain some creative insight after, then go for it and get those words on paper. Just remember to edit them after with a clear head. We offer editing services too, just in case you don't have the time to go back over the 50,000 words of drunken meanderings you've written!

WHERE DO YOU DO YOUR BEST THINKING?

You'll have found this with your businesses already, but where do you do your best thinking? Many people resolve an issue overnight while sleeping, so it's always good to have a notebook by the bed ready to jot ideas down in the morning, before the day takes over. Some of my best thinking happens in the shower.

Having previously been in the police, the murder manual advises senior officers to take a break; go for a walk. Looking up and away from the paper for a bit can unlock the brain in so many ways, and quite often after half an hour away, things get solved faster than spending hours staring at the paper.

Think about what works for you, and make a note of the inspiration that came from it.

NOTEBOOK TO HAND

Always have a notebook close to hand, that great thought will have gone by the time that you next come to write. Then you'll likely spend your half an hour trying to recall it. Keep a notebook by your bed, in your coat pocket, in the car, on your desk, and when the inspiration comes, jot it down, even if the idea doesn't make it to print, at least it saves you half an hour trying to think of what it was. Let me know if you find a waterproof notebook for the shower!

VOICE NOTES

Would these work better for you than writing them? If so, go for it, record your thoughts, and then when you sit down to write next time, use these to guide your writing.

USE WORD TO TRANSCRIBE

Transcription services have come on leaps and bounds over recent years. If you gaze in wonder at touch typists and wish you didn't type like a dinosaur with fat fingers, you may find that dictating straight into Word works best for you. Just click the dictate button on the toolbar and away you go.

SCROLLING/GAMING

We're all guilty of it, sometimes it's useful for various moments in your life, sometimes you strike upon some inspiration or gain solace from it, but have a think about whether there is some time that you spend scrolling FB or playing that game that you love/hate playing that you could cut down on and use for your writing instead. You may even surprise yourself and find the 3 ½ hours a week here!

WHEN IN THE ZONE...KEEP GOING

If you are in the full throes of writing, keep going, so long as you can. Think about how long it took to get into the zone, to be unstuck, to start writing. And now you are there writing, ideas keep coming, and the words keep going onto the page. Use this time for as long as you can, even if you set yourself the task of writing for 30 minutes, if the writing is coming, keep going. Imagine what you will achieve during this time. You may well far exceed your target of 500 words or even 3,500 words, giving yourself more time later in the week/month, or getting your book written sooner. Stay at it and keep going.

YOUR GOALS, SMART OBJECTIVES

You've likely used these in your business or for other tasks, so use them in your writing too.

Write down your goals for your book, for your session, what you're going to achieve by the end of the session, week, month, and year. Apply this to your writing. There's a template to download for your writing on our website here:

writingdr.com/resources/

WHAT WORKS FOR YOU IN BUSINESS WITH YOUR TIME MANAGEMENT

Simple one here, you are successful in your business, you manage your time effectively when working, so think about how you do this and apply this to your writing.

CREATE TIME

We've talked about how long you spend scrolling FB or playing that game that you love/hate playing, but how many other things are there that you do that could be done more efficiently, or that you could think about your writing while doing them? As mentioned, my best thoughts often come while showering or going for a walk.

HOW DO YOU EAT AN ELEPHANT?

For some, sitting down to write a bestselling book could be a mammoth task, so break it down into smaller tasks, focus on what you are going to achieve today, during this writing session, and ignore the larger part of the project for a moment. Just sit for 30 minutes and write. This will likely resolve any imposter syndrome or writer's block that have crept into the project.

If you've settled down for an hour and are thinking, 'How am I going to write 1,000 words?', break it down. Set yourself a 15-minute target of 250 words. Go for it now, write out your why, 15 minutes, 250 words. How easy was that? Then go again and again...and again and voila 1,000 words have appeared without you even thinking about the wordcount.

Or in other words, you eat an elephant one bite at a time.

MUSIC

What music helps you write? What music helps you focus?

I have found that different types of music have really helped my creativity and focus on the project.

Classical music allows me to concentrate fully on the task in hand, while house music allows me to quicken my writing pace. What works for you? Or is it silence? And if so, how do you create this to block out the distractions?

The golden ratio, 1:1.618, or Phi has been used throughout the course of time by mathematicians, scientists, artists, architects, and musicians, including Pythagoras, Johannes Kepler, Salvador Dali, Fibonacci, Leonardo da Vinci, Mozart, and Beethoven. It is linked to improving the power of concentration. which is why Classical music is often used when studying or concentrating on tasks.

Some examples of pieces which include this to listen to:
Mozart's Sonata n. 1 in C Major
www.youtube.com/watch?v=ZixdOZh7zo4
Beethoven's Fifth Symphony, first movement
www.youtube.com/watch?v=B7pQytF2nak
In for the long haul, over 11 hours here:
Mozart Effect Make You Smarter, Classical Music for Brain Power, Studying and Concentration
www.youtube.com/watch?v=6CMKa119hFA

WARM UP!

What gets you in the mood? Plan something that will get you in the concentration/writing zone. You can incorporate this into your writing routine on a daily basis. Some ideas:
Light a candle
Meditation
Cup of coffee/tea
Breathing exercises
Re-read the last page you wrote, revisit your SMART plan
EFT... Emotional Freedom Therapy

EFT

Emotional Freedom Therapy (Tapping therapy)

Stick with me, because it really works.

This was first demonstrated to me while I was in the police during covid as a coping mechanism for stress. I have subsequently seen teams of firefighters, businessmen, and the NHS use it during the pandemic, and it has been demonstrated on the Chris Evans breakfast show.

Try the below as your warm up, but you may also find it helps throughout your daily life and has been used successfully to help those with PTSD and chronic pain.

The theory behind it is that it reduces your cortisol (stress) by releasing beneficial chemicals through your body.

The first time I did this was in a room full of police officers, you are more likely to be by yourself, unless you're reading this on a train, so there's even more reason to give it a go.

Choose what you want to let go/think about.

How stressed are you? How much pain are you in? How much is it bothering you? How much are you stuck?

We'll focus on writing, but you could use it for stress, anxiety, problems, and pain.

F ollow this guide or watch the You Tube video:
Ready...
Tap hand continuously –
Say 3 times
"Even though I only have 30 minutes – I'm going to write 500 words"
Then follow the below, saying "Even though I only have 30 minutes – I'm going to write 500 words"
Tap top of nose/between eyebrows
Tap next to the eye
Tap under the eye
Tap under the nose
Tap under mouth, above chin
Tap collar bone
Tap under 3" under armpit
Tap top of the head
Tap top of nose/between eyebrows
I'm ready to write
Finding time and energy to write
I'm strong, grounded, and focussed
Right now
Ready to write
Then write away.

For a guided EFT session please visit: www.youtube.com/watch?v=kglRchnxBDI

ENJOY WRITING

Embrace the writing time, start to look forward to the time when you can write, we all get more done, work better and more efficiently when we enjoy it, and this will come across in your writing. Find the right time for you to write, learn about your energy and when is your optimum time to write.

Reward yourself, like the warm up, how are you going to reward yourself for your writing? While report writing in the police, a cup of tea when I pressed send on a file to the CPS was incredibly rewarding, as were the guilty pleas and sentences that followed.

WRITER'S BLOCK/PROCRASTINATION

OK...so none of the above has worked or you're completely stuck, but you've sat down for half an hour and only have that time, and nothing is coming. What are you going to do? Because you need to do something. Don't lose this time! Fine, the 500 words might not hit the paper right now, but can you do something else? Anything? So long as it is to do with your book project, don't go off scrolling FB or playing that game that you love/hate playing.

Use the time to update your SMART plan for your writing, or for planning your next couple of writing sessions, is there some research you can be doing? Is there a quote or idiom you want to include in the book, but can't recall it exactly? Search for it, find out who said it, is it true? "Write drunk, edit Sober" as Hemmingway didn't say.

By following a myriad of the above I have written 2258 words (1st draft) in an hour and 56 minutes, I enjoyed Mozart, I enjoyed writing it for you and consumed no alcohol or elephants but three cups of tea and am now heading off for a rewarding pork pie.

YOUR WRITING STYLE

Everyone's writing style is unique. It's like a fingerprint. You probably noticed that the last chapter is a little different sounding. This is because it was written by Peter. Frankly my time management is gloriously chaotic, Peter may have a different way of describing it. Anyway, everyone's writing style is different. I can tell you who wrote what, simply because of their writing style. Back when I taught Chinese students how to write essays, I could have a class of 40 and still identify whose writing I was looking at. You might think you write like everyone else, but you don't.

I'm a dreadful judge of character when it comes to face-to-face meetings, but I'm pretty damn good when it comes to the written word. This also means that when people send me AI-written stuff and try to pass it off as their own, I can usually tell by the end of the first paragraph. This is because people's souls show in their writing, but when AI writes, that soul is absent. It's the weirdest feeling, reading something which doesn't have a fingerprint. It's unnerving, and at some level, this must be felt by more casual readers. I'll be speaking about this later. Right now, I want to tell you that your writing style is important.

Take a look at the writing style of books that are in your field and identify which books you find effective, and which you don't. If, while you're reading, you start daydreaming about Finland's 1976 entry to the Eurovision Song Contest and a gallon jug of peanut butter, then it's not written in a style you should emulate. Damn those sexy Fins and their Pump-Pump song. They were robbed at 11th place.

What you may find is that nowadays people like to read business books that sound like they're being spoken to. So, adopting a more talkative style can work wonders. If you're used to giving talks, then use that style in your books.

Remember:

It helps sometimes to add in punchy short sentences to break up long paragraphs.

Try writing your opening paragraph in a few different ways to choose a style that works best. What gets your message across effectively? You may be writing about something highly professional, but every reader needs a bit of drama or levity.

Don't lose the you behind your words, but do adopt successful tactics of other writers.

As the late great Fredi of the 1976 Finnish entry sang:

'You gave me the pulsating spark of my soul.'

A sentence that is so wrong on so many levels, but also somehow utterly, bizarrely wonderful.

It's okay to be you.

Just make sure you're the interesting, readable version of you.

Key Takeaways:

- What is your writing style?
- Which style of writing do you like/dislike?
- Make it engaging, conversational

- Does your writing sound like you?
- Try different styles, which do you prefer
- Be You! That's what your readers are reading about you for!

ENGAGING YOUR READER

There's one thing the professional writer knows that the first-time writer often overlooks.

You have to write in a way that engages your reader.

You may desperately want to write like Joseph Conrad, but unfortunately, if all of your audience is reading Fifty Shades of Grey (or whatever the newest trashy, smut-filled bestseller currently is), then you won't get far.

I'm not saying you need to include leather chaps and whips in your books about Paraguayan Trade Union Laws, but I am saying you need to take note of the style people like to read.

When eBooks first came out, I remember being told that publishers thought it would make more people read highbrow, weighty tomes, such as Vanity Fair and War and Peace, because those books were previously considered too big and difficult to carry on the Tube.

But you know what happened?

People quit reading highbrow literature altogether and started reading more bodice-ripping smut. Because when you have an e-reader, nobody can see the dodgy front covers starring bare-chested moustachioed men with swooning heroines clinging to them while their clothes unravel.

As someone who has given her life to literature and writing, I don't know whether to find that disappointing or hilarious. Indeed, there was a stage in my life where, upon finding out what I did for a living, everyone would ask if I had read 50 Shades of Grey.

Everyone.

From suited and booted professionals to pub landlords, to senior civil servants, to my own flipping GP. Heck, even my gynae wanted to know.

The answer is no.

No, I have not read 50 Shades of Grey.

I have, however, had my sister, after a few glasses of wine, phone me up to read out some of the worst sentences that book has to offer, whilst cackling like she's in a scene from Macbeth.

Truly a Wyrd Sister moment.

And that was quite enough 50 Shades of Grey for me. In fact, I dare say it was too much.

So, what does that all tell us?

Aside from the fact that my GP has terrible taste in books?

Well, it tells us that most people don't really want great literature. They don't want beautiful language, metaphors, similes, themes, tropes, and exquisite descriptions.

They want to be entertained.

With your business and coaching books, they want to learn important information and vital skills for work and life, but they also want to be entertained.

And what is that dreadful phrase that is always so horrendously misused?

The customer is always right on matters of taste.

The first-time writer can typically become a little self-indulgent and expect people to read their book because it contains serious and great ideas.

The professional writer knows you have to earn your audience.

And how do you earn your audience?

You write engagingly.

There are so many ways to engage your audience in your book. And trust me, none of the suggestions I'm about to make include BDSM nightmare fuel.

Use humour, drama, sadness, happiness, life stories, use acronyms, point out where other people have failed. All of it is entertaining.

First, get your reader on your side. If they like you, they're more likely to keep reading and listen to what you've got to say. We looked at this in the chapter 'Your Audience Wants to Know You', but it's worth discussing a little further.

I want your audience to feel like you're on their side. Like you're cheering them on. They should feel supported by your book.

If you're going to say something like:

'The next step is difficult and hard work.'

Add some encouragement to it, for example:

'The next step is difficult and hard work, but I know you can do it with my help.'

Be kind to your reader; build them up and let them know they can succeed. Where appropriate, show them how you managed it and the obstacles you had to overcome to make it through. They'll feel more understood, and they'll feel more like success could be a possibility than if you tell them, 'Well, I was born brilliant and everything I've touched since turns to gold.' And believe me, I've read enough books that unfortunately do this to know it's a surefire way to make your reader hate you.

So let me take you back to my first writing job. I was working part-time as I was in the process of finishing my PhD. I put my profile up on a writing website advertising my expertise, but nobody would hire me due to a lack of feedback.

I was therefore ripe for the picking by a client who seemed to never use the same writer twice...

A red flag I was too green to notice.

He asked if I could write action. I said, 'Of course.'

And so, he employed me to write him a short story where a femme fatale beats up a bunch of useless henchmen.

'Fine,' I thought. 'Easy enough.'

However, each time my first client had me adjust a scene, it got gradually more...well, the first thing he wanted was for her to wear thick, tan-coloured tights. Then he wanted her shoes to fall off. Then he wanted her feet to be sweaty and for some of the unfortunate, or perhaps fortunate if this sort of thing swings your bag (things got weird fast), henchmen to be suffocated by her aforementioned sweaty, tan tights-clad feet.

And there went my first freelance writing job. At that point, I was Nicola Russell Johnson BA Hons, MA, MPhil. Not yet Dr., but still qualified up to the eyeballs in writing. And I was writing for this terribly polite, well-paying, strange, little pervert.

It was not at all the way I envisioned my writing career to start.

What happened, however, was that he gave me an absolute belter of a review, and with just one person's endorsement, I suddenly started receiving offers for some utterly wonderful writing jobs. History, biography, business, academia, artistic fiction, self-help books, you name it and I'm sure I've done it at some point.

That lovely little pervert did come back to ask me to write for him again, and while I owed him greatly for triggering the landslide of clients that I got to pick and choose from, I told him he was better off with a specialist...

So, what's the takeaway here? It's that it's okay to be human in your book.

People like humans!

So do tell your origin story. If your career stems from some sort of passion, let your readers know! If you had a tough start, people love an underdog! This book could be your superhero origin story. Is there an exciting reason you became a quantity surveyor? Let us know!

This is your book; you control the narrative here. You can use that to get your readers on your side. I studied WW2 in depth for my PhD, and one of the many books I read was Albert Speer's Spandau Diary. And because he is controlling the narrative, you actually start liking the guy. He includes this cute story about Christmas gift-giving with Hitler. It's the weirdest thing. You actually start thinking he's just a nice man who was in the wrong place at the wrong time. And you continue to think this right up until the moment you stop reading and close the books and realise he is Albert Speer, the monstrous, Nazi, psychopathic architect.

So, if Albert Speer can convince the reader that he's a well-meaning, sympathetic character, then I have no doubt, dear reader, that you can represent yourself well in your books. After all, you're not a Nazi war criminal, I hope.

Back to it. Inserting moments of your life is a great way of engaging your reader. So, tell them (where appropriate) of your highs and your lows. Tell them of funny moments and scary moments. And use these moments to teach your techniques to the reader. Let them enjoy your successes with you, and help them to look forward to their own successes with the help of your book.

If they trust in you, then they'll trust in your services. And you'll be able to properly help them.

If, however, you present yourself as untrustworthy or as not a particularly nice person, you'll find your audience less receptive to your advice. They'll be distrustful of your company, and they won't take the relationship of author and reader to the next level of company and client.

If this makes me sound a little mercenary, let me just tell you that before I work for anyone, I do a little bit of research on them first. If they look dodgy or give me an off feeling, I refuse the job.

I have seen business books that take the opposite route, although I'm suspicious it wasn't done on purpose. One particular book comes to mind where the title and strapline make outrageous promises of the money-making opportunities within it. It starts off with almost a hundred pages just on his childhood and young adulthood. He tries to portray it like it was a terribly hard childhood, but actually, it was a pretty average childhood. He wasn't rich, but this seems to be the only hardship I could determine. By page 50, you're getting antsy to get to the bit where he tells you how to make money. By page 75, he's done questionable things, and you find yourself disliking him thoroughly.

Now, I daresay what he was trying to do was tell people that he managed to do well for himself despite such a tough start in life and some terrible decisions. He's hoping to inspire people with this, but unfortunately, his upbringing wasn't hard enough, and you don't get the feeling that he's a nice enough guy to want to see him succeed and become a millionaire. I know the angle he was trying to push, but it didn't quite work. This is why (unless you're writing a flat-out autobiography) you keep the little peeks into your life fairly short and disperse them amongst the important information you want to share.

ACRONYMS

Acronyms abound in business and coaching books. Don't go overboard, or they'll fail to be effective. Think about when and where you find acronyms useful in your work life. If you don't find them useful in other people's books and talks, then don't feel like you have to use them yourself. When done well, they can really help you negotiate tricky situations. When done badly, they can make my eyes roll so hard I can see into last week.

There's nothing worse than an acronym that desperately wants to fit together to make a dynamic word but is a bit too forced and unnatural.

So here is a helpful acronym to teach you and help you remember the rules of using acronyms:

Never overuse acronyms.

If in doubt, check with a colleague.

People won't remember them if you use too many.

Practical. Be practical and don't force information in just so you can spell a good word.

Less is more. Don't make your acronyms too long.

Everyone is using them, but that doesn't mean you have to, too.

Sausages.

There. So, the next time you think about using an acronym in your books, stop for a moment and think **NIPPLES**. And nipples are sensitive things, so use them sparingly.

THE OLD DICTIONARY DEFINITION THING

You know when you're in a meeting and you notice everyone else writing something down, so you draw a bunch of little pictures in the margins of your notebook to try to look busy?

Sometimes I think the business book version of this is shoving in a bit that says something like:

The dictionary defines the word 'hackneyed' as this:

Hackneyed [**hak**-need]
Adjective: commonplace, done before or trite; stale; banal.

I'm not going to mince my words here. If you even think about using this in your book, you can get in the bin (although take your laptop in with you so you can carry on writing your book minus the Dictionary definition).

I want you to think about the last time you saw a professional use this, in a book or an article or a talk. How did it make you feel?

Did it make you want to jump out of your seat with excitement?

Did it make you want to make a mental note of it because it was so good you wanted to tell your mates down the pub about it after?

Or did it make you think, I already know what the word entrepreneur means, Nigel, now get on to something interesting?

The old dictionary definition thing is an example of writing that is just thinking of filling more pages and not actually thinking about what the reader will enjoy.

Even if the definition is something quite different to what people expect, you're better off just saying, most people think bla means bla when actually it means bleuuugh.

Pretty much everyone who sees that dictionary definition bit is thinking that the writer is procrastinating because they need to fill pages. Nobody dances for joy when they see them.

For example:

The dictionary defines procrastination as:

Procrastination [proh-kras-tuh-**ney**-shun]

Noun: the act of putting off and delaying something that needs to be done right now, Julia.

STRUGGLING WITH A BORING BIT

Now, if you need to write an informative section that's just going to have to be a little dry, if there's no way to spice it up with an interesting anecdote, then it's okay to just flat out tell the reader. It's okay to say, 'Stay with me here, this part might be a bit heavy going, but it's totally worth it, I promise.'

This seems simple and obvious, but so many people don't do this. And when I say this, I don't mean to do it like the shampoo adverts that say something along the lines of 'Now for the sciencey bit' in a manner that suggests all the women watching couldn't possibly care or understand about science. Don't patronise me, shampoo advert.

What I mean is, it's okay to say, 'I need to be serious now' or 'this part might feel a little bit dry, but it's absolutely vital you read it' and other versions of this. If the reader thinks that it's just going to be for a short while, they will absolutely keep reading, especially if you tell them why it's important they read it.

Right, I'm going to leave you with a last acronym on entertaining and engaging your readers:

Most people will read the dullest subject matter if you make it engaging.

Oxford Dictionary definitions are no-go and don't go overboard with acronyms.

It helps if you get your reader to like you.

Superlatives work well, your highs, your lows, and your finest moments.

Tyrannosaurus Rex

Key Takeaways:

- Engage your reader!
- Write for your reader
- Get your reader on board for the journey
- Guide your reader through the book, especially the heavy-going sections
- Be You! Show some obstacles you faced, highs, lows, successes
- Tell your story
- Use acronyms effectively, don't overuse them (NIPPLES)

YOU KNOW YOUR GRAMMAR REALLY

Now, I know I've spent the last chapter telling you that you should try and get your audience to like you, but this chapter is going to be a 'do as I say, not as I do' moment.

Because I'm going to say something which will probably make a bunch of you not like me all that much.

I bloody love grammar.

I do.

I really do.

If, however, just the thought of grammar makes you panic, fear not. You're in the majority. And what's more, it's not your fault. UK schools did not properly teach grammar for a long time.

I wasn't taught grammar either.

In fact, I had to learn it when I became an EFL teacher and went abroad to teach English. And on the teaching course, we weren't even really taught grammar. We were taught how to teach grammar effectively, but we weren't taught the actual grammar. Hence, my panic when on my first day as a teacher, I was asked about the past participle and its usage in the third conditional.

You'll be pleased to know that my understanding of grammar has greatly improved. You'll also be pleased to know, I'm no longer a brand new, green teacher; in fact, I'm turning really quite grey.

That Valencian school was a baptism of fire from all angles. Mornings, I had a class of five-year-olds who were the most feral children I have ever come across. I shall never forget the day one boy came in after standing in dog poo. He took off his shoes and started walking them up the wall, leaving dog poo prints. When I was rushing over to stop him, three kids ran out of the classroom, and one kid in the corner pulled his trousers down and started yelling something in Spanish while gesticulating wildly at himself. Another kid spat on the doorknob of my now swinging open classroom door after the three runaways had cast it aside. At that moment, the headmaster walked in to see what the heck was happening, just as the little girl next to the boy with his bum out had had enough and kicked him squarely in the nuts. I then look back at the headmaster, who grabs hold of the doorknob to stop more kids running out, just to realise it was covered in gob.

That class was my Vietnam.

And I don't think anything has managed to ruffle me since.

Where was I?

Oh yes, grammar.

Right, there may be some of you out there who are fearful that your grammar might be a bit dodgy. After all, who amongst us has not at some point mixed up 'fewer' and 'less'? Who amongst us hasn't had their 'they're' autocorrected to 'there' and sent the text without noticing?

And I shall never forget my utterly wonderful sister-in-law at the age of 14 scrawling 'YOUR STUPID' on her brother's notebook.

(I will return to my sister-in-law later, because she's awesome and can teach us all a little lesson in resilience that will be pertinent when talking about reviewing and editing your work. Honestly, you won't believe what that brilliant weirdo did, and where she did it.)

Okay, here's a list of common grammatical issues people have. I'll subtitle them so you can skip over mistakes you're confident you don't make. If you skip over all of them, congratulations! Your grammar is better than half of the people who write shop and café signs up and down the country.

THEY'RE/THERE/THEIR

These three words sound the same but have different meanings.

THEY'RE - This just means 'they are'.

For example:

'They're laughing at me because I forgot to take my socks off at the swimming pool.'

THEIR – This is a possessive. Use it to talk about ownership.

For example:

'They ate their sandwich quietly, then they scoffed everyone else's.'

THERE – This is used for everything else. Notably, a place.

For example:

'My new house is over there behind the dumpster.'

'There you have it, cold fusion using a Meccano kit, three elastic bands, and a copy of Ken Dodd's autobiography.'

YOU'RE/YOUR

Again, these sound the same, but are used differently.

YOU'RE – This just means 'you are'.

For example:

'You're an expert in the field of Barry Manilow.'

YOUR – This is another possessive. You use it when something belongs to you.

For example:

'Is this your puncture repair kit, or does it belong to your girlfriend?'

FEW/LESS

So many people use less for everything, even when it's grammatically wrong, that I dare say the English language will change to make it acceptable. At the time of writing of this book, however, it is not grammatically correct, so get it right!

The difference between few and less is all to do with countable and uncountable nouns.

A countable noun is anything you can count, for example, trees, tractors, and traffic wardens.

When you are talking about a countable noun, you use 'fewer', not 'less'.

So, you might say: 'I wish there were fewer traffic wardens in Milton Keynes.'

You use 'less' when talking about things you don't count, for example, water, bread, or butter.

(Now I know there are times when it may be acceptable to use these words as countable, but take a look at this and see how weird it feels:

'Would you like two or three breads for your sandwich, and how many butters would you like on your toasts?'

'How many waters have you drunk today?'

It's just not right, is it? You need to say how many 'slices' of bread, or 'glasses' of water, before you can put a number with it.)

So, when you are talking about something you don't really count, you use 'less', for example:

'I wish you would put less water in my Pot Noodle.'

'I need to eat less bread; it's making my ankles swell.'

ME/MYSELF/I

Most of us will remember being corrected as a kid for saying something like 'My friends and me went to the park', because it should be 'My friends and I went to the park'.

The easiest way to work out if it's okay to use 'me' in a sentence like 'Me and my mates got dinner' is to take out all of the other people and just reduce it to 'me', like this:

'Me got dinner'

See? It doesn't work. So that tells you that your sentence should be:

'My mates and I got dinner.'

Because, as you can see, if you take out your mates, it still works: 'I got dinner.'

Another way to know when to use 'I' and when to use 'me' is this:

'I' does the action.

'Me' has the action done to them.

This means it's: 'she said to me' and 'I said to her'.

Or in the words of the late great Victoria Wood:

'Smack me on the bottom with a Woman's Weekly.'

And:

'I could handle all the tenors in a male voice choir.'

MYSELF

Misusing 'myself' is a new sort of trend, and it's not as fun as it sounds. People who use 'myself' incorrectly are usually trying to sound professional, such as:

'This book was written by myself.'

Now I know it's not the done thing to tell one's readers to get in the bin twice in one book, but if you use 'myself' like this, go ahead and get back into the bin.

If you're unsure of how to correctly use 'myself', then avoid it. Nobody will miss it.

But if you really must use it, then here is how:

You only really use 'myself' for emphasis. Do not use it to indicate the subject of the sentence (the subject of a sentence is the person carrying out the action). If you use 'myself', you must also include the subject in the sentence.

Take a look:

'I wrote this book.'

The subject here is 'I'.

If you want to add 'myself', it looks like this:

'I wrote this book myself.'

It works with himself, herself, yourself, and themselves.

So you can say:

'You read this book yourself.'

Or:

'She wrote her book herself.'

But never do this:

'This book was written by himself.'

Or:

'The battery in this van was replaced after using a multimeter to diagnose the electrical system, by myself.'

When you use 'myself' incorrectly in speech, it's not a huge deal, not really. It's not possible to be perfectly grammatically correct when speaking all the time. People don't mind. However, if you use it in your writing, it's the equivalent of putting milk into your Earl Grey. Darling, don't do it.

<u>WAS/WERE</u>

Now, I'm sure you know when to use 'was' and when to use 'were'.

'Was' and 'were' are the past tenses of the verb 'to be'.

Once you know that, it's hard to go wrong. It goes like this:

I am --- I was

You are --- You were
We are --- We were
They are --- They were
She/He is --- She/He was
It is --- It was

There are some regional dialects that incorrectly (in terms of grammar) say 'I were' or 'It were'. For example:

'I were talking to Bernard the other day.'

If this is how you speak because of your regional dialect, then carry on my wayward son. Accents and dialects should be protected and cherished at all costs. But don't write them in your book, got it?

Another section of grammar some regional dialects get wrong, are perfect tenses. So let's have a quick look at them.

PERFECT TENSES

There are three perfect tenses. The present, past, and future. The future perfect isn't used very often, but you cannot escape the present tense, it has got itself everywhere.

THE PRESENT TENSE

An example of the present tense is this:

'I have just given a talk on Gloucester Services Southbound.'

Note the use of 'have' and the verb 'to give'. When we use perfect tenses we must use the past participle, which in this case is 'given'.

Give – is the present simple
Gave – is the past simple
Given – is the past participle

Now, how many times have you heard people say:

'I have just gave a talk on Gloucester Services Southbound.'

It's all the time isn't it! Also, Gloucester Services is brilliant.

There are a few verbs that people often misuse when using the present perfect. Take a look at these erroneous sentences:

'I have just spoke to her the other day.' (Needs to be 'spoken'.)

'I have went there three times.' (Needs to be 'gone', but note 'been' also fits.)

'I have ate breakfast already.' (Needs to be 'eaten'.)

All of these sentences I have heard and indeed in many places they are the standard way to speak. I will defend regional dialects with everything I've got. I cannot stand the homogenisation of the English language. But when it comes to your book, please write it correctly.

THE PAST PERFECT

The past perfect looks like this:

'Claire had already been stopped by a police officer and given three points on her license before she had held her license for two months.'

(And by Claire, I mean me. I'm a terrible driver.)

You can see here the past participles being used 'been stopped' and 'held'.

Here is how bad it looks when you get it wrong:

'Claire had ate all of the pudding before her husband had finished his main course.'

(And by Claire, I mean me again.)

There is one verb which people sometimes struggle with. And it's drinking. People struggle with drinking.

It goes, drink-drank-drunk

So: 'Claire had drunk all of the wine before her husband got home from work.'

(Honestly, that Claire, she's terrible.)

FUTURE PERFECT

This isn't used very often at all. It looks like this:

'By the time her husband gets home, Claire will have drunk all of the wine.'

(Is this giving you Tiger Who Came To Tea flashbacks?)

Again, you need the past participle.

Right, you lovely lot, let's move on to a bit of punctuation.

Punctuation can be a little bit harder than grammar, because with grammar, you have the option of reading your work out loud and feeling when it's not quite right. Take for example, these sentences:

'My mate was going to take myself to town but they had drank too much at lunch and a ticket was gave to himself.'

Just reading it hurts, doesn't it. And it's pretty obvious that it should be:

'My mate was going to take me to town, but they had drunk too much at lunch, and a ticket was given to him.'

With punctuation, however, aside from commas and full stops, it's not so easy to hear when you've gone wrong. Plus, some punctuation errors are so damn ubiquitous in modern life, it's not hard to get confused. How shall we start? Shall we begin with apostrophes?

Let's.

APOSTROPHES

Apostrophes are actually very simple to use; however, people get a bit slap-happy with them.

The main reason to use an apostrophe is for possessives, which means it indicates when someone owns something. For example:

'You are reading Nicola and Peter's book.'

'I'm not keen on Janet's wallpaper.'

'The canteen's coffee should be a criminal offence.'

Sometimes people freak out if the word already has an 'S' at the end or is a plural. In this case, stick the apostrophe on the end.

'James' cooking is the worst I've come across.'

'Flamingos' knees are actually their ankles.'

Now, how simple is that? Whatever you do, don't have a panic attack when pluralising a word and shove an apostrophe in, which is famously seen on the signs of shops and markets across the UK. For example:

'Parsnip's 50p.'

'Free cookie's with every cup of tea.'

If you are even thinking about it, then you need to step away from the apostrophe. It's not needed!

This bit is a little obvious, but I'd be amiss if I didn't mention it here:

You can use an apostrophe to replace the 'O' when you contract words such as 'do not' to 'don't'.

See also: Can't, won't, shan't, and their past tense versions didn't, couldn't, wouldn't, shouldn't, etc.

THE EM DASH

Before AI started writing everyone's social media posts (and Lordi help us, sometimes even their books), the em dash was only ever really seen in classical works and contemporary romance novels. Now people have started spotting AI use due to its absolute overuse of the em dash; there are some who are starting to defend it. Indeed, some of them claim they have always used them prolifically.

My advice is to leave the em dash to the romance writers.

I have no idea why AI is so fixated on them. Perhaps AI loves a bodice ripper, I don't know. However, I do know it's perfectly possible to write an entire novel (as long as it's not romance) without even using a single one.

Think back to when AI wasn't a thing. Did you use them that often? They're nothing really that can't be replaced by a comma or a nice set of brackets.

In fiction, you can use them for interrupted dialogue, that's when they really become useful. Outside of that, in contemporary non-fiction writing, there are few times when you really, really have to use them.

Sometimes I think the way AI writes is having more of an impact on the way we write, than we are impacting the way it writes. Who is learning from whom?

If you really have to use an em dash, then go for it. Don't use them with any great frequency though, they'll detract from the overall readability of your writing and will have people second-guessing if you're a robot or not.

THE SEMICOLON

The semicolon is in great decline, and I can see why, but it's still a bit of a shame. You use a semicolon in places where a comma isn't enough of a pause, but a full stop is too much:

'I tried to be healthy today; unfortunately, the wine caught me at it.'

You can use a semicolon also when a sentence has two clauses:

'I went to the gym once; my muscles are still writing to their local MP to complain.'

You can also use them when you use nevertheless or however:

'He swore he could fix the sink; nevertheless, we now have to swim to the kettle.'

And you can also use them in lists:

'I have only ever wanted three things in life: an end to poverty; world peace; and a fourth season of Ash vs Evil Dead.'

If you're unsure, you can generally just use a comma, but a semicolon is always nice to see; so don't shy away from them completely.

Now, Word does a pretty good job of highlighting errors in red and blue. So, if, when you've finished typing, your document is full of little red and blue lines, check it! The same goes for your emails, but then I'm supposed to be teaching you how to write a book, not how to write to the complaints department of your local supermarket about their increase in prices and their manipulative use of shrinkflation. Although, quite frankly, I'm well up for that too.

Finally, if all I have done is muddy your cerebral waters when it comes to grammar and punctuation, you can just leave it, write however you want to write, and then come on over to Writing Dr and we'll fix it up for you.

Because after all?

We just bloody love grammar.

EXISTING
MATERIALS

The chances are that you use social media to promote your company and yourself. I'm not saying you post duck lip pictures of you standing in front of national landmarks while tourists queue up out of shot for their turn, I mean, maybe you do, and if that's the case, you do you, love. Some of those photos look incredible. What I'm saying is that you probably have already produced a lot of content, and this could help you when writing your book.

Think about it, one chapter should be roughly 1,000-1,500 words long. That's a blog right there. Remember the chapter 'It's Your Time, Use It'? That started off life as a blog Peter wrote for our website and was included in this book to demonstrate how to use your time and your existing materials cleverly.

Have you written newsletters? You might find you've got another chapter right there.

I've already spoken about noting which social media posts gained the most interest and traction. Use these as part of your toolkit, too. Perhaps the biggest existent materials you might have in your arsenal are the talks, webinars, or presentations you've given. After all, and I know I'm repeating myself, an hour of talking gives you about 18,000 words.

Using content you've already written, spoken, or posted online can help you to establish your voice and to be consistent with it. Repurposing social media posts can stop your writing from being overly pretentious or stuffy. It can be easier to get your personality across on social media than it is when gazing into the abyss of writing 30,000 or more words.

So, have a little look at everything you've done so far, if you've done public talks or podcasts and you've not recorded them, dredge up your notes on them. If you've written blogs, newsletters, courses, emails, and anything else, use them!

Don't, however, use any of those social media posts where you make it look like your dog is talking and saying things like 'I woof my mummy.' Let's leave those behind and pretend they didn't happen.

Your book, is then the perfect launch pad for your next round of social media posts, newsletters etc. Just use it the other way around and utilise the content of your book for your media.

Many people then use their book and the chapter plan to create their own courses. The content of your book can be expertly turned into a course for your learners, with the book then accompanying this course.

We just so happened to write an English course for pilots and air traffic controllers during our time as English teachers, each lesson carefully planned, with resources and materials, and this easily then became a course book to accompany it, but of course it would work equally well the other way around.

Key Takeaways:

- Re-purpose your content

- Use your blogs, social media posts, newsletters as ideas and a starting point for chapters
- Record your webinars, meetings, transcribe this and use in the book
- Re-purpose your book for your social media content, newsletters etc.
- Use your book to design your own courses, with your book acting as the coursebook

CASE STUDIES

When it comes to business, case studies are a great way to validate your work. They do a couple of things: they demonstrate to your audience that you're good at what you do, plus they make what you do a little less abstract and a bit clearer. If your reader can see themselves in the people you talk about helping in your case studies, even better. It'll help push the idea that what you do works and can work for them, too.

Make sure your case studies are about times you've done a reputable job for reputable people. This isn't the time to talk about working for a man who had a thing for stories about being squeezed to death between a robust lady's thighs while wearing sweaty tights.

It's a good idea to use your case studies to show that you can help a range of different people with a range of different problems that you and your company can solve. If you have an ideal client, then using case studies is a great way to get them to identify how much they need your help and how great the outcome could be if they work with you.

Now, are case studies the most entertaining and engaging of things? Not really, but they are incredibly useful, and I encourage you to put some in your book, because whether your reader is the sort of person who reads the case studies, or if they skim over them, they demonstrate that the ideas within the book, and your overall expertise, do actually work. Those people who skim them are still impressed by the idea that your work isn't just theoretical, it's functional. It shows people that if they take your advice, they'll achieve whatever it is they bought your book to achieve.

A great case study is one that is specific, it doesn't just say:

'Dr Nicola Russell Johnson is a lovely person to work with.'

A great case study tells a little tiny story. It starts at the beginning, with a pain point or a problem or a need. It talks about working with your company, and it delivers a happy end, where your company fixed everything, had favourable outcomes, and delivered everything your client wanted and more.

Let's look at how that structure looks within an actual case study:

'Client X knew he wanted a short story about a female assassin in sweaty tights, but his own attempts to write it were amateurish. Client X called us and gave us an outline of his story. We took it from there, we were receptive to all the changes and additions needed, and voila! The story satisfied the client and was exactly what he wanted to the point he attempted to come back a second time.'

Let's have a look at a particularly interesting client I worked for. I can't go around naming my clients because I'm a ghostwriter, so instead, let's call him Shirley.

'Shirley was an extremely big fish in a very specialised pond. Even if you've not heard of Shirley the person, you'll absolutely have heard of the historic event associated with him. Shirley is famous enough that when they emailed me to ask if I would write his book, my first question, which I asked in a rather starstruck way, was, 'Are you that Shirley?'

Shirley's problem was this: everyone was writing books about Shirley. However, Shirley himself had no book and therefore no real voice. Shirley wanted to get their voice and their story out. However, Shirley had no experience writing books and no time in which to do it. Shirley came to me with their story and their materials, and I conducted my own research. We had the book out and published in a matter of months. It ended up being published in three languages, and I see them on television fairly regularly. Books are still being written about Shirley because Shirley's story is fascinating. But out there, shouting above the din of all the other books, is Shirley's book. The one that tells the real story.'

So, the order here is Shirley's problem, my solution, and the happy ending. You can see the pain point and how I was able to fix it. Anyone who wants their book done quickly and professionally in order to place their own authority above the crowd can see how Writing Dr can sort it out for them, painlessly and efficiently.

It's a good idea to use your case studies as evidence to prove you can do what you say. Don't go overboard on them, because while they contain useful information and can be persuasive to potential clients who may be on the fence, they're not the most engaging things to read. You want your clients to know what you can do, but you don't want them to start skim-reading. However, don't leave them out altogether. Sometimes what your company does can sound a little abstract, case studies turn the theoretical into reality. It's a chance to show your reader what your company looks like when it's in action.

Key Takeaways:

- Validate your work, add credibility
- Ensure case studies are reputation enhancing
- Use a range of case studies, clients, services
- Demonstrate what you do works
- Use them to back up the chapter/point you are making
- Use them to break up the book, separate sections

CLARITY

Okay, so you've got a plethora of ideas.
Okay, so you're brilliant at what you do.
Okay, so you're Brad Pitt.

Well, sorry Shania, but actually two of those things do impress me much. It doesn't mean, however, that all of them should go into the one book.

If you're struggling with a tangential muddle, it's time to bring some clarity back to your book.

Planning your book before writing it can help. It's the blueprint for your house, it's the skeleton underneath your skin, it's the trellis supporting your wisteria. I'll stop now. Let's bring some clarity to this.

First, I want you to think about your book and its purpose. What will it teach the reader? How will it benefit the reader? Why should someone read your book?

Second, when you plan your chapters, decide what you want your reader to take away from each one. Try and really narrow it down, so you have a clear purpose.

Once you have a firm plan, don't lose sight of it. If you want to introduce new ideas, think first if it will stop your main message from coming out clearly. Would those new ideas be better off in their own chapter or even their own separate book?

So, we've got a clear idea of what you want to write and what message you want to impart. How else can you achieve clarity?

Well, let's talk about the writing itself.

When you discuss a concept in your book, a great way to stop it from being too abstract is to use examples that inform and elucidate. This is a great time to use those case studies we talked about. It's also a lovely spot for your own personal experiences.

Sometimes an idea can be hard to understand until a little bit of storytelling makes it nice and clear. If your case study or your personal story is entertaining, then in one fell swoop, you've educated and entertained your reader. Perfect!

If a case study or a personal experience doesn't fit into what you're writing about, it's okay to write hypothetical scenarios to bring clarity to your point. Take care with them, though; they're brilliant for explaining how things work, but they're often not brilliantly entertaining, and you may find certain types of readers skim or skip them.

Another way to bring clarity to complex ideas is to do a breakdown of steps to show your reader how your process works. This is a good way to unravel complicated systems, techniques, procedures, and practices.

What I also want you to look at is the wording of your book. It's a rather tired old trope that business-speak includes a lot of 'putting pins in it', 'thinking outside the box', and 'brain dumping'. 'Pivoting' seems to be a big one right now, and I personally can't hear it without thinking of Ross getting his sofa stuck in the stairwell.

If your entire book hinges on a particular business phrase, let's use 'pivot' for example, then absolutely use it and feel free to use it with frequency. However, if you overuse business-speak that is not integral to your book, it can get a bit too much. Your message may not come through clearly enough; it may even give your readers the impression that you're not fully sure of what you're writing about. It may appear as if you're purposefully muddying the waters to hide a gap in your knowledge. Or, for the sake of clarity, it may seem like you're being vague or obtrusive to stop your readers from spotting your weaknesses.

So, go easy on the old jargon. I'm not telling you to cut it out completely, just make sure your readers can understand you loud and clear.

I'd like to talk a little about metaphors next.

Metaphors are okay, but they're a bit like wedding invites. You might spend hours picking them to get them perfect, but the recipient probably won't notice if they're embossed or on matte or shiny card. They'll just scribble the date onto their calendar and chuck them in the bin.

A nicely placed metaphor, such as my above example, can help, but often they can be a bit redundant. At worst, they can be annoying.

The second problem with metaphors is that AI loves them.

Now, AI is getting better all the time and no doubt will one day become indistinguishable from real human writing, but right now it still has a long way to go. There are various telltale signs, such as the overuse of em dashes, dull, lifeless writing, and flipping metaphors. AI loves to say things like, imagine your book is an arrow and your perfect client is the bullseye, you want to be able to hit them every time...or something like that. I don't hit my clients, I promise.

So, before you use a metaphor, check that it's needed. Think whether a case study or a personal or professional experience wouldn't work better. And don't use too many. I've seen AI books that like to use a new metaphor every chapter and then practically beat the reader to death with them. Which one is it, AI? Is digital marketing like an elevator that hits every floor, like a carefully made tiered wedding cake, or like four wrestlers in a Ford Cortina? Pick one and stick to it!

So, I'll leave you with this metaphor about metaphors:

Think of them like doughnuts. One or two here and there are delicious, but too many will give you diabetes, and you may end up losing a toe.

Key Takeaways:

- Plan!
- What is your book's purpose?
- Who is it for?
- What will it do for you?
- What will it do for your reader?
- What are the key takeaways of each chapter?
- Read your book as though you are the reader, is it clear?
- Would a case study assist?
- Would an image, or link to your website work better?
- Jargon – is it needed? Is it relatable and understandable to your ideal client?
- Metaphors – do they help or hinder?

CHATGPT WRITE MY STORY!

I have dedicated my life to the written word. I'm not saying that's a particularly good thing. One of my dearest friends has devoted her life to cancer research, and while I write better sonnets, I can't help but wonder at my life choices when I'm around her.

Where was I?

Yes, I have dedicated my life to the written word, and now there exists a computer programme that can not only write, but it can write in a matter of seconds. You know that bit in Charlie and the Chocolate Factory where Charlie's dad's job of screwing the lids on toothpaste tubes is taken over by machinery? This was how I felt when AI became a writing tool, that is, until I looked more closely at it.

As it currently stands, AI cannot do the job a human writer can do; in fact, I'm going to make the argument here that even bad writing done by a human is better than AI writing.

I shall start, however, by saying nice things about AI, because while I may seem like a hater, I'm not. Not completely.

For blogs or social media posts, heck, even newsletters, AI can level the playing field for people with dyslexia or other issues that make writing difficult. Content is king right now, and I absolutely love that AI can be used in the same way one might use a wheelchair or a pair of glasses. It is an aid to people who would otherwise struggle. And for that, I shall always support AI and its development. Anything that can help create equality for people with disabilities is A-okay in my book. I also support the usage of AI for people for whom English is a second language. Your success shouldn't be limited just because the English language likes to play silly buggers with irregular verbs.

I bloody love an irregular verb.

When it comes to writing your book, AI can be useful. It can help you plan somewhat and give you ideas on structure and order.

I think that sums up what I think AI is pretty darn useful for.

So now, the bad bits.

I know it must be tempting to get AI to write your book. After all, it can be done in minutes. And after all, writing is my love, not necessarily yours. Getting AI to write it might feel like the best way to get your book done painlessly, cheaply, and quickly. There may even be some of you out there thinking that by entering all your information into AI, the book it then produces is technically all your work. There's even a chance that there are those of you right out there at the back who think, 'I'm wasting my time any time I write because AI can do it faster.' After all, AI can write in different styles, can't it? And you can programme it to use a style specific to you!

Well, listen, I'm going to shut this down right now.

In terms of the writing itself, there are issues that I think are huge red flags, but, dear reader, you may not be all that bothered by them, so before I talk about how badly AI writes, I'm going to give you the biggest reason you shouldn't use AI:

AI uses every source it can find on the internet to write for you. This probably sounds great; your book will come from the accumulation of information from thousands of minds. However, there is a massive drawback, and this is such an important point I'm going to emphasise it by making it a standalone line:

AI can and does sometimes lift entire sentences from other people's work.

What this means is you may have a whole book written in mere moments, but then you may also end up with a lawsuit from some professor in Stow-on-the-Wold who's had their PhD thesis on marketing plagiarised. And you don't want to mess with a Stow-on-the-Woldian; they can get nasty.

I imagine now that for a large portion of you, that's all you need to know to step away from the AI. But I'm a writer! I want to have a little rant about all of the other reasons AI writing is no good. So, rather like a choose-your-own-adventure book, feel free to skip to the next chapter. However, should you want my professional opinion, tie yourself to the mast, because I'm about to unleash a storm.

Here's the thing about AI. People, usually people who don't read all that much (which is fine by the way, there are plenty of books out there that shouldn't be read), think that AI writes just like a real human. That it's indistinguishable from the writings of a real person. Well, here's the deal:

I can tell.

I can tell when it's AI, and a lot of us out there can. In fact, I was given a business book just last week and asked my opinion on it. All I had to do was flip through and pick out odd sentences here and there to know it was written by AI. It may as well have been written in dayglo pink; it's so very obvious.

I'm quite sure AI will get better and better. It may well get harder to distinguish it, but for now, it's pretty obvious.

To start, it's kind of unreadable. And when I say that, I don't mean it's a bunch of nonsense, because it's not. In fact, em dashes aside, it's usually punctuation-wise and grammatically correct. But it doesn't yet understand that people have to read it, so while it may or may not be factually correct, it's spectacularly dull and sort of hollow.

Now, I really wanted to show you exactly what I was talking about by including a section written by AI. However, if we went ahead and put it in, we'd then have to disclose that we've used AI to write our book and potentially fall foul of copyright and plagiarism. So instead, please do check out the blog on "Should You Use Chat-GPT or AI to Write Your Business Book? Here's What You Need to Know (Written by AI)"
www.writingdr.com/should-you-use-chat-gpt-to-write-your-book/

Spoiler... it tells you not to!

So, it's not bad writing, per say, but it has no life to it. It would be hard work to read a 50,000-word book of it. Trust me, I've done it. It's like, and Lordi forgive me but I'm going to use a bloody metaphor, you know those people who decorate their houses in nothing but beige? Then they wear beige, and their children wear beige, heck, even their kids' toys have to be beige. That's not what I call bad taste; it's what I consider to be a lack of any taste whatsoever. And when people decorate their houses in a manner that looks like Cath Kidston threw up all over it, at least that is some kind of taste, which in my mind, is infinitely better than having no taste at all.

AI writing is like that beige house. Give me Cath Kidston's barf any day of the week.

So, whenever I struggle to read a book (bearing in mind I read several a week), I know it's been written by AI. And so far, when I run it through a checker, I've been right. In the future, will this continue to be so? Who knows? I am asked regularly if I will take on decently paying jobs where I teach AI how to write better. I always refuse them, but there may be some superb writers working on it as I type this.

So, what is it about AI that makes it a struggle to read? Let's take a look.

We all know that AI loves em dashes and metaphors, but there are deeper issues. AI doesn't use personal/professional experiences to engage, entertain, and elucidate. This means its writing is as dry as something they used to refer to as Ghandi's flipflop. I'm not sure what the kids are calling it these days. And it goes further than being a little dry; there's simply no life at all behind the writing.

Whether you know it or not, everyone's writing is a little bit like a fingerprint. Even when people write using professional or academic language, that fingerprint stands out. It's the reason why forensic writing analysis is a thing. It's the reason I could tell who had written what when I worked teaching Chinese students how to write essays. The first time I was given a book to work on that was written by AI, I knew there was something wrong before I even started the second paragraph. This is because the writing held no fingerprint at all.

It was creepy as heck.

Have you heard of the Uncanny Valley effect? It's a very cool concept that, as far as I know, nobody fully understands. It all started with robotics. When you make a robot that doesn't look like a human, nobody has a problem with it. Then if you start to give it a face, but it's an overly cute and not very realistic face, people start to quite like it. However, when you make that face human, only just a fraction off, people freak out. Things that look very nearly human are creepy as heck, eerie as heck, and sort of revolting as heck.

The Uncanny Valley effect is what you feel in that scene in Men in Black when the man/alien blinks and his eyelids go sideways, not up and down. It's when you look at pictures of Momo with her mouth that's a bit too wide. It's how you feel in the film Signs when the alien walks past the window. If you're a human, it hits hard, and it seriously gives you the willies.

Nobody has come up with a definitive reason why we get so damn weirded out when we see something that looks human but isn't quite, but the theories people have come up with are seriously fun.

1. Maybe it's to signal to early humans that Neanderthals were a different species from us, even though they were sort of similar.
2. Maybe it's ingrained in us, so we feel scared and avoid people who are dead or who potentially carry a contagious and life-threatening disease.
3. Maybe it's a primeval warning to avoid psychopaths who perhaps display very slight indicators of emotions that are violent. Think the whole 'smile doesn't reach the eyes' sort of thing.
4. This is my favourite. Maybe thousands of years ago, aliens who looked almost like us, but not quite, walked among us and were highly dangerous.

I love a good alien conspiracy. That is, I love them when they're not spreading some kind of political agenda.

Whatever the reason, we all experience Uncanny Valley when something is so very human, but not quite.

Well, dear reader, when I read stuff written by AI, I get Uncanny Valley. Now I know, I know, I deal with writing every day, so of course it will impact me, but I can't help but feel that the layman, when reading AI, can feel there is something, however faint, a bit off.

Now, there may be some of you shouting, but AI can write in so many different styles!

1. If you're shouting at a book, your neighbours might start worrying about you.
2. When you ask AI to write entertainingly, it invariably just sounds like something out of Women's Weekly.

You don't want to sound like Women's Weekly, do you? No shade to Women's Weekly, my grandma used to love it. But you want to sound like you. I know you do. Stop arguing.

There is also an interesting thesis to be written on the way AI is potentially impacting the way humans write. If people continually come across AI writing in their social media, in their business posts, and even in AI-written books, they will start to adopt AI's style. Then we will have a vicious circle of who is informing whom, and I fear that good writing may be the ultimate victim.

So, AI overuses the em dash, it overuses metaphors/similes, and it has no human interest behind it. There was, for a while, on social media, a calling out of writing that used em dashes, because it's a pretty clear sign that AI has written it. There is now a pushback from people claiming they love the em dash and have always used it.

Things may change, but right now AI loves the em dash. AI loves the em dash the way Multi-Level-Marketers love emojis. They love it more than people from Milton Keynes love sharing your lost dog notice on Facebook.

There are just certain ways of writing you associate with certain demographics. And I'm afraid em dashes will, for a goodly amount of time at any rate, be associated with AI.

Things will change I'm sure, and we'll all go back to barely noting their appearance.

Has your em dash run away at the park in Aberdeen?
Shared in Milton Keynes, hun.

Key Takeaways:

- Do NOT get ChatGPT to write your book
- Even ChatGPT agrees!
- Use AI to help you plan, review, bounce ideas off... but don't let it write it for you
- You are the expert in your field – your reader wants to hear you
- When publishing you have to indicate that AI has been used
- AI will take things straight from your competitors
- You will fall foul of copyright and plagiarism
- AI writing is hard to read – how many social media posts do you skip straight past because they are clearly written by AI and not engaging?

WRITING COACH VS GHOSTWRITER VS AI

WRITING COACH

So, you know you want a book, you don't want to dither over it for years, but you're not really sure how to get one done.

I get it. It's a big project, or at least, it can feel that way if you've not done it before.

A writing coach might be the answer to your struggles, so what can a writing coach do for you?

Well, a coach can help hold your hand and guide you step by step through the process, if they're a good one, that is.

A writing coach can start right at the beginning with you, from your first 'I want to write a book but I'm not completely sure what to write about' thoughts. They can help thrash all of your ideas out and order them into the structured plan of a book. This is something people don't utilise enough. They go away and think about their books for a few years, and then come to a writing coach when they know what they want to write about.

This is the same thing as cleaning your house before the cleaner comes round.

A coach's job is to help you plan it, as well as help you write it. A coach can help you identify all of the parts of your books that work really, really well, so you can replicate that technique throughout your book. They can help fix any pacing issues. They can help you clarify parts, and help you make other parts more entertaining. Plus, they can help you find your voice.

At Writing Dr, your coaching includes proofreading and editing, and as I like to say off the record, general fixing up of your book.

A writing coach is a bit like having a little cheerleading squad, although I don't think it's a good idea to hand me pompoms. We will encourage you every step of the way. When writer's block hits, and let's face it, there's a good chance it will, we can help you write yourself out of it.

There are lots of coaches out there, all of whom offer different levels of service; some, for example, won't proofread your work for you. Many firms will hand your manuscript over to random freelancers, although no shade to freelancers, many do good work.

So, if you choose to write your books with a writing coach, make sure you pick one whose services are what you need.

We are very hands-on at Writing Dr. Peter is an accredited coach, so he has excellent interview skills to help you get your ideas out and onto the page. Nicola, or as I'm the one writing this particular bit I should say 'I', I work through your words with you. If you struggle to articulate something, I'll do it for you. If you find it tricky to create suspense and engagement, I'll show you how.

So, if you can write and you're up for the challenge, but you're not too sure how to go about it, a writing coach could be the perfect thing for you.

GHOSTWRITER

Some of the biggest names out there have books on sale that are ghostwritten, and there are several reasons why it might be right for you to do the same.

The first and foremost, I think, is when you just don't have the time to write it yourself.

If you're writing a book because you have a successful business and you want to push it to the next level, chances are you're already up to your eyeballs in work.

You might even have put a day aside to write, got a few words down on the page, when an important call comes through, and now you're no closer to getting your book done than you were last month, or last year, or even further into the past. This is when hiring a ghostwriter can really be a good idea, especially if all you have to do is call them up and chat about it. Imagine that! Just chat to our coach, Peter, here at Writing Dr, who sends the transcripts to me, and I'll turn it into a book. And, as the French entrant to the Eurovision Song Contest 2021 says, 'Voila!'

Another good reason to get a ghostwriter in is when you're starting to notice your competitors releasing publications. If you need to beat your competition and you need to do it fast, a ghostwriter can get it done for you. And not just done, but done well. Any good ghostwriter will also research your competitors' work, and help give you an edge over them.

Yet another reason to get a ghostwriter in is to do with ability. Maybe you're a master at sales, maybe you're a scientist, heck, maybe you're the head of a successful charity, but writing just isn't your strong point. That doesn't mean you don't deserve a book. And it doesn't mean people don't deserve to read what you've got to say. Get a ghostwriter in! They'll be using all of your ideas, all of your knowledge; they'll just be getting those words down on the page for you. Don't let your lack of writing ability stop you from having a book. Your ideas deserve a platform as much as the next guy.

Hiring a ghostwriter is a surefire way to actually get your book written. It's a way to get your daydreams of having a book made into reality. Plus, you'll get a professional product at the end of it.

<u>AI</u>

Again, I've read quite a few books that have been written by AI. By the time you read this, I'll have probably read even more. They are the literary equivalent of unseasoned rice. However, I can't deny, it's a wickedly fast way to get a book written.

AI is perfect if you want a book simply for the sake of having a book, and perhaps more importantly, you don't actually expect anyone to read it. This is the perfect scenario for utilising AI to write an entire book, as long as you're fine with parts of it potentially being plagiarised.

I find AI to be dull, repetitive, and just a little bit creepy. I also find myself instantly disinterested in any body of work that I know has been written by AI. Has anyone started to read a story on Reddit about some entitled person stealing a window seat on a transatlantic crossing, only to get halfway through and realise the constant use of em dashes and the overly short paragraphs mean it's written by AI? When I reach that point, I don't even bother reading on.

Life, real life, is interesting.

Digital regurgitation of fake stories is not.

Now, after having said that, there are absolutely ways in which AI can help you write. If you're struggling to structure your book, get AI to help you write a chapter plan. You can go through it after to add your personal touches to it. AI can totally aid you when it comes to ordering your ideas, and it can throw a few of its own into the pot, too.

In terms of the actual writing, however, don't use AI. Heck, go ahead and ask AI if it thinks you should use it to write your book. It's going to say no.

Getting it to help you structure your book, though? Go for it.

Key Takeaways:

- Writing Dr coaching can help you overcome the enormity of the project of writing a book
- Writing Dr coaching can help you work out the book's purpose and how you can use it to enhance your business
- Writing Dr coaching can help plan your book, get started writing, overcome writer's block, cheerlead you
- Writing Dr coaching can help you with the reviewing, proofreading, formatting, and publishing of the book
- Writing Dr ghostwriting can help get your book written and fast when you don't have the time or ability
- Writing Dr ghostwriting will do all the research for you
- Writing Dr ghostwriting will interview you, using a combination of detective and executive leadership skills to draw out all the information about you, your story, your business, and products and services
- Writing Dr ghostwriting will write it up to a PhD level of writing in your voice, engaging your ideal client, and making it a book that will enhance your business
- AI will give you a book...potentially one that falls foul of copyright and plagiarism, and one which is highly unlikely to be an engaging read for your ideal client, possibly causing you reputational damage
- AI can help you with planning, can help you with editing, and with reviewing, but this will then need checking!

Check out Writing Dr's services here: writingdr.com/services and book a call with Nicola and Peter to see how we can help you get your book written and fast.

REVIEW: HOW MANY DRAFTS?

There are a few common pitfalls that lie in wait for first-time writers. A major one is to write the first chapter over and over, desperately trying to get it right and never getting any further. I come across this all the time, and it's a rookie mistake.

By all means, play about with your first couple of paragraphs to get the tone and voice right, but once you've got a fixed idea of the style you're going to use, get writing and don't look back until you've finished the book. If you need to go back and change things, okay, go ahead, but don't get stuck in a loop of doing the same small section over and over.

When you've completed the book, that's your first draft done.

There absolutely needs to be a second draft. If the first draft is written well, your second draft may not have any major changes in it, but it's useful to look out for any sections that fall flat, or could be written better, as well as taking note of the moments that work really well. This way, you can further emphasise the good bits and use those techniques to potentially improve the dodgy bits.

Going over it a third time, is for polishing it up to perfection.

However, there are many successful writers who write dozens of drafts, and their books change massively from the first draft to the last. So, I'm not going to put an exact number on it. I will say an absolute minimum of three.

I shall let you into the secret of my writing process. I plot my books down to the last detail. This takes, on occasion, longer than the book takes to write, which means that when it comes to the writing of it, I won't have to make any changes to the structure in later drafts. This is a huge help. Restructuring an already written book can be a massive process.

Once my book is all planned out, I write it, by hand, in a notebook. Whether the book is 30,000 words or 92,000 words. I handwrite it. This is something I recommend, but I also understand it's not for everyone. When you write by hand, your mind can focus more clearly, as it's not also having to work to find the keys to type. Neither is it distracted by all the little red lines that invariably crop up on the screen (I'm a fast and slightly inaccurate typist).

The second benefit of writing by hand, is that when something is no good, you can draw a line through it and carry on.

This is important.

It is vital to see what has gone wrong, so that you don't do it again. You may also sit down to write on another day and realise that the crossed-out part was actually on the right lines, with a bit of tweaking.

If your first draft is on a computer, all of this would have been deleted and never seen again.

My second draft happens when I'm typing up my written manuscript. This is when I spot if a comment is too abstract or if a section needs more drama or further clarification.

My third draft is a read-through of the typed text. This is where I correct any small errors, and it's the first time I read it as if I were seeing it for the first time.

Finally, before signing off on it as a finished piece, I do a last run through for any stray typos.

So that's how I do it.

It's not entirely for the faint of heart. Writing hundreds of thousands of words a year means my right (writing) hand generally curls into a fist involuntarily due to writer's cramp, but it works for me.

For some people, the thought of typing up 30,000 handwritten words can be a little too daunting, and that's fine. Although, you can overcome this by typing out each chapter after you handwrite it.

Whatever the method you use, your first draft won't be the finished article. Be prepared to have to run through your book at least three times.

A way around this, of course, is to hire out someone else to do it. I can certainly help craft a finished article from your rough first draft, and sometimes an outside eye can help spot what needs to be done better than someone who has been immersed in their work for a long time.

So, how many drafts should you do?

Well, not too few and not too many.

There, does that clear things up for you at all?

You're welcome.

Key Takeaways:

- Don't review, review, review at the expense of writing, writing, writing
- Work on getting a first draft written
- Then look at reviewing and a second draft and so forth
- Plan before you write

- When reviewing seek to clarify, add or remove more to enhance your writing and messaging
- Review to correct small errors, typos, try and read it as though you are reading it for the first time

SELF-EDITING VS A FRIEND VS A PROFESSIONAL

The benefit of editing your work yourself is that you can get your manuscript edited the way you like it. The benefit of getting a friend to do it is that it will be edited the way your mate would like it. And the benefit of getting a professional to edit it is that it will get done right.

Before you even think about giving your mates your work to edit through, you should have a damn good go over it yourself. Nothing makes a colleague feel like a big man more than when they're slathering your work in red pen. So, if you have the time, edit yourself first.

There's a good chance, however, that you will miss things. There should be a word for it, like a Freudian Slip, only a writer's version, where you know what your manuscript should say, and so that's how you read it, even if it says something different. We should come up with a name for it now. My favourite author is Philip K Dick, so in honour of him, shall we call it a Dick Slip?

All of this is to say that no matter how diligent you are, it can be tricky to spot all of your own mistakes. What's great about a friend is that it's a fresh pair of eyes on your manuscript. They can help to show you any parts of your book that may not be clear enough. Sometimes, when you know your subject well, you can make assumptions that everyone is following you. You may skip basic steps or move too quickly through a process that other people need longer to grasp. A good friend will let you know you've done it, so you can rewrite the section to be more easily understood.

A good friend will also tell you which parts they enjoyed the most, so you can go back and emphasise these, or use the same techniques elsewhere in your book.

All of this is brilliant help.

But it's not without potential problems.

If your good friend isn't a writer or a big reader, they might suggest changes that simply won't work. A friend of mine, who is a graphic designer, often deals with customers who know nothing about graphic design but who have an awful lot of opinions anyway. He'll do a design for them, they'll say, 'Great, but change the colour, the layout, the font, the overall shape, and the style.'

And then when he does, usually with a polite warning beforehand, they'll look at what all of their suggestions have created and say, 'Well, now it looks terrible!'

Of course it does!

They haven't spent years studying graphic design at university. They haven't actually got a clue what they're talking about. I like to compare it to when a toddler insists on applying your makeup. It's always going to end in disaster. This is exactly the sort of issue you may encounter when asking a mate to look over your manuscript. They may have a bunch of suggestions, but you're going to look like a two-year-old did your eyeshadow if you pander to all of them.

The most help a good friend can be is to tell you which parts they enjoyed, which parts they didn't, which parts they drifted off during, and if there are any parts they struggle to understand. And even then, you need to make sure you've picked the right friend. Because we all know there are those 'friends' out there who quite like pushing you down. You know the ones; everyone has had one once. The ones that will do anything to feel a bit superior to you, the ones that sabotage you a little. The ones with a bit of an ego problem. These sorts of 'friends' will gleefully cover your manuscript in red pen, despite the fact that they haven't got a clue what they're talking about. They'll invent issues where there aren't any, just to feel like a big shot. And this can really bring you down and stop you from achieving your goal of writing a book, which is exactly what they want.

So, if you're going to have a friend cast an eye over your work, pick your nicest friend; the one who always supports you and lifts you up.

The one option that doesn't involve any pitfalls is to go to a professional. If there is something not quite right about your manuscript, they'll be able to pinpoint what it is, why it doesn't work, and how to fix it. They'll be polite, they'll be an expert, and you'll know you can trust that their advice is sound. They won't try and alter your book if it's already good, they won't use criticism to one-up you, and finally, they'll want your books to be great because it will now reflect on them if it isn't.

Here at Writing Dr, if your manuscript is a banger, we'll tell you it's bloody brilliant. If it's a great topic that is executed drearily, we'll show you how to bring it to life. And if, and when, I break out the old red pen, it won't be because three years ago you suggested my living room carpet looked like something you'd find in a North Macedonian airport lounge, and I'm looking for revenge. And that's because, not only do I have nine years of university education, including a PhD behind me, not only do I have over fifteen years of experience helping people write their books, but I also fully accept that my front room carpet looks like it belongs in a North Macedonian airport lounge, and I like it that way.

When you come and work with us here at Writing Dr, you'll get two people, who on top of everything else were teachers of English as a foreign language for over eight years, teaching grammar, punctuation, and all things writing. Both of us were International English Language Testing Systems (IELTS) Examiners, grading students writing. This gave us a real eye for reviewing work and looking for the kind of error we may find in a 2nd or 3rd draft.

I continued working with students around the world on their writing for many years, helping them to get the grades they need to study and work abroad. We're talking business professionals, medical students, and doctors who needed to pass to be able to work in Australia, Canada, the US, and the UK here!

Peter was then a detective in the police, not only scrutinising evidence and reviewing colleagues' submissions to partner agencies, SLT, Crown Prosecution Service, but also reviewing complex cases with many many more words than your business book, looking for typos that could make a whole world of difference, this included when a typist had written up an interview omitting the word not...

"Clive said he did do it!"

This didn't half trigger a moment of euphoria where we all thought that we had cracked the case with a full and frank guilty admission! When it emerged it was a typo, we all learnt the importance of triple-checking all documents with additional vigour.

What the above means for you and our clients is we can spot a rogue apostrophe from a million miles away. A typo jumps off the page at us! So, your work, when published, will be error free, enhancing your brand and reputation.

Key Takeaways:

- Choose your reviewers with caution. Which mate/colleague will add value or use it as an opportunity?
- Check for Dick Slips
- Fresh pair of eyes
- Spot the typos
- Can others follow your writing? Is your reader on the journey with you?
- Writing Dr will be professional, polite, and will give you sound advice you can trust
- Nicola and Peter can spot an error from three blocks away; ensure your reviewer/proofreader can too!

Ready to have your work reviewed? From time to time, we offer a free 1,000-word review, check if it is available today at writingdr.com/resources or book a call with us to discuss how we can help you get published.

EDITING - PROOFREADING - FORMATTING

You may think that the writing part of your book is the hardest part. You may think that when it's done, all of the grunt work is over.

Well, think again!

Let me introduce you to proofreading, editing, and formatting.

So, I've talked about the pros and cons of proofreading and editing yourself vs a mate or a professional, but I've not really talked about how you get on and do it.

One of the most common ways to proofread and edit, is to read your words out loud. This will immediately highlight any errors or sentences that don't flow well.

Feel free to use your computer's spell checker, but remember, you don't always have to take its punctuation advice. It's not infallible.

EDITING

Right, what exactly is editing? This is when you evaluate your book in terms of clarity, accuracy, order, and engagement. Does each chapter discuss what you want it to? Does it make your points nice and clear? Is it engaging to read?

Look out for any awkward sentences.

Make sure the tone and the voice are consistent and appropriate throughout.

If you haven't taken my advice and planned your book cleverly in advance, then the editing stage is when you'll have to pay for it. You may have to restructure your books, rearrange chapters, add chapters, or change the information if it's inaccurate. None of these things are impossible and even with a nice, crafted plan, sometimes professionals find they need to do some heavy lifting in their editing stage.

If you didn't check your sources, claims, dates, or the people you are going to quote in your planning stage, get it done now.

If, while writing, you got a little carried away and found yourself waffling, the editing stage is the time to cut it down (although well-written waffle can sometimes be a thing of beauty).

PROOFREADING

Proofreading is similar to editing, but it's where you get down to the nitty-gritty. This is where you'll look for any spelling or grammar issues. While you're fixing any typos or spelling mistakes, check your punctuation too.

If you're of an age, you might automatically add two spaces after a full stop here and there. It's only one space nowadays, the kids aren't down with two (it's also because we don't use typewriters anymore. I mean, you might, and if you do, fair play to you). So, the proofreading stage is when you sort that out.

Another thing to look out for when you're proofreading is the unintentional repetition of words. It's totally okay to repeat a word if you're doing it for emphasis, style, or rhythm, but not if it's by accident. So, if you use the same word twice or more in too short a space and it stands out, get a thesaurus up on your phone and fix it. Now, I don't want to name or shame anyone, but I worked with the loveliest client, absolutely adorable, who kept writing sentences like this:

'The project progressed slowly, largely due to how slow it was.'

'The team collaborated together on the proposal to ensure everyone was working collaboratively.'

This kind of repetition doesn't work.

Repetition that is done purposefully works beautifully. Think about Churchill's 'We shall fight on the beaches' speech. Or even better, think about Sojourner Truth's 'Ain't I a woman?' speech.

You may not enjoy proofreading particularly, but do not skip this stage at any point. Too many errors in your manuscript will leave your readers highly unimpressed, and this will lead them to doubt the content or become so ticked off that they quit reading altogether. Want it done professionally? Come on over to Writing Dr and we'll sort it for you. I can spot a double space from six paces away, depending on whether I've misplaced my glasses or not.

FORMATTING

This is the job everybody hates. I mean, even I'm not keen on it. The editing and proofreading stages are still creative and exciting. You're making your book better and better. But with formatting, there's no creativity to it. It's just something you have to do, and you have to do it right!

Formatting is all about how the words on the page look. We're talking page layout, font choices, spacing, margin settings, chapter headings, subheadings, tables, charts, graphs, headers, footers, paginations, bullet points, footnotes, endnotes, citations, etc.

Or at least, you'll be talking about it with Peter, because that's his domain. I'll just say this before I hand you over: if you don't format decently, your book will look pretty bloody awful, and that can put a reader off faster than opening up your book with a dictionary definition or a quote from a convicted criminal running a Ponzi scheme. So, get it right, or get Peter to get it right for you!

Key Takeaways:
- Try reading it aloud to check for errors and clarity
- Are there any inconsistencies in your writing, both with the content and the voice?
- How does the book read?
- How does the book flow?
- Are the chapters in the correct order?
- Check sources, dates, quotes, claims, and case studies.
- Cut out any waffle
- Add in any clarity
- Check for any repetition
- Would another word/phrase work better?
- Ensure your writing is spot on and error-free, the book is to enhance your writing, not put off a potential client with too many errors

FORMATTING WITH PETER

It's a pain in the bum! One false move, or even a right move that somehow randomly changes with the printing house, and your whole manuscript is out of sync.

Whilst a pain in the bum...you want to ensure you get this right. You've spent a lot of time and money, and are showcasing your knowledge, experience, and expertise, so you want to make sure your ideal client reads a polished, error-free book, which reflects you and enhances your personal brand. So it is worth the time, and potentially money if you go with an editor or publisher to make this perfect, to get your book looking good.

It takes some fine-tuning to ensure your book is looking perfect both in manuscript form and then when published on paper in your hand, and often a little tweaking is required at the submission stage to ensure it is just right.

If doing it yourself, you will discover that the various print companies will all have their own slant on how to do it, but the general rule is to upload your document in Microsoft Word. For this reason, and for the industry standard, this means most agents, publishers, and editors will also request you submit your document in Word.

Writing Dr are no different, Word please.

Having the document in Microsoft Word is also useful when in the editing stage and when toing and froing a document with your editor or publisher, as they can leave comments and track changes.

When submitting the document, look to follow the guidelines presented to you by your publisher or editor; many will refuse to look at it unless you have. If you're not doing this yourself, please feel free to skip the next bit, and if you are doing it yourself, brace for the dry bit of the book, and enjoy the formatting experience!

If you are doing it yourself, you should look at the size of your book and then ensure that your Word document is the same size. Pop onto the "Layout" tab, then select the "Page Setup" and click "Size". Then select the page size according to the size of your book.

To ensure that the margins are correct, go back onto your "Layout" tab and select "Page Setup" then "Margins". Once in the margins, select "Mirror Margins" in "Pages" from the "Multiple Pages" drop down and then "Whole Document" in "Preview" from the "Apply" drop down.

FONTS

Go with the standard ones. If you want something to look fancy, point this out to your editor or publisher with a note, explaining what and why, but for the most part, in the book, go with your standard fare and stick to this throughout.

So, fill your creative boots with "Arial", "Times New Roman", "Calibri", or "Aptos". These are the ones you will generally find as your default on Microsoft Word, so you shouldn't really have to do anything here, aside from not touching anything.

And whilst you're not touching anything, leave the alignment to the left and stick with 12pt and black.

CHAPTERS

Put a page break in at the start of the chapter and put the chapter title in as "Heading" style. This will help when you come to do a table of contents.

TABLE OF CONTENTS

Once you have all your chapter titles as "Heading", you can then create a table of contents with ease. Simply click on "References" and then click on "Table Of Contents" and choose "Automatic Table 1". Click back in and select "Custom Table of Contents". Then de-select "show page numbers". This will take all the page numbers away... don't worry, the printing company will add these in, but if you put them in when submitting, the numbers could all be on a different page number when it goes to print!

And click on "Show Levels" and select "1", this will then just show your headings. If you wish to have sub-headings, select "2", but we'd advise with keeping your table and book clean, and just going with the heading, before your Table of Contents becomes a mini book in its own right.

HEADERS AND FOOTERS

In your header on alternate pages, have "Author" in the top left of the left page and "Title" in the top right of the right page.

In your footer, have the page numbers, in the bottom left on the left page and bottom right on the right page.

If you would like a template for your manuscript, either before you start out, or when you are ready to publish it, please do feel free to book a quick call with us, and we'll happily provide you with one for your book and happily guide you through the final stages.

writingdr.com/book-a-call

FRONT AND BACK MATTER

Your book is going to start with a Title page, which should be on the right and on the first page, so the reader sees it as they open the book.

There would then be the Copyright page, which would include the date first published, edition number, author and publisher details, and details about the rights of the book.

You may wish to include dedications.

You would then have the Table of Contents.

At the start of the book, you should then look to include a Foreword, then getting straight into your book with a brief introduction.

At the back of the book, you should look to include an "About the author" page; this should be on the right-hand page. If you have a bibliography, this would again sit on the right at the back.

Key Takeaways:

- Get someone else to format it for you!
- Good luck if doing it yourself!
- Enjoy the formatting experience!

SOME REVIEW
GUIDELINES

When you are reviewing your book, and when you are getting feedback, I want you to be resilient. You don't have to respond straightaway to feedback. Have a think about it first. If, when you are reviewing, you're not keen on what you've written, don't let it destroy you. Be stubborn, remember why you wrote the book, and keep battling through it. This is where I'm going to tell you about my wonderful sister-in-law. My wonderful sister-in-law joined up with a group of people to climb Kilimanjaro for charity. In the group, there was, I believe (she'll correct me if I'm wrong, I'm sure), a bit of ribbing going on. Some of them thought my sister-in-law wasn't going to make it to the top. I dare say this was because she is a little bit of a glorious nutter, and people who are not that bright don't notice she has a backbone made of titanium. Her plan, and this may go towards people underestimating her, and why I just called her a glorious nutter, was to take a space hopper with her and be the first person to space hop on the top of Kilimanjaro.

So, they set off.

One by one, the people in her group dropped out, because it was such tough going. And it is! It's bloody hard going. Before long, my sister-in-law was the only one left still climbing. She then had to join another group. However, this group was of more experienced climbers, and they were decidedly unfriendly to this delightful little weirdo, who didn't seem to be taking it seriously and wasn't quite the same calibre as them. They were even worse than her first group when it came to telling her there was no way she was going to make it to the top.

Well, she made it.

All the bloody way up.

With her space hopper.

And quite frankly, if that is not a lesson in resilience and sheer stubbornness, I don't know what is. Would she have made it to the top if people hadn't kept telling her she wouldn't? I don't know. When she puts her mind to something, she doesn't quit.

Now I want you to think of what you are going through when someone says they're not keen on part of your book, or if you realise the second half doesn't really work.

You can just keep working on it.

You can just type out more words.

It's not climbing Kilimanjaro with a space hopper.

I might make that the name of my next book....

Right, so now I've told you to all be good and resilient, here is a bit of a checklist with some review guidelines. It's not going to be the most interesting or the most fun chapter of the book. But hey ho, at least it's not climbing Kilimanjaro with a space hopper.

So, here are some big questions to ask when reviewing your manuscript:

- Who exactly is your intended audience, and have you catered to them? It's no point using an abundance of expletives if

you're writing for Mormons (I was going to say the W.I., but heck, they'd love it).
- Does your book stay on track? Does it focus on its core purpose, or does it wander around aimlessly? A bit of an aside can be fine, as long as you don't stray too far from your point. Some people, and you know who you are, skim everything (probably even this). They could skim Jane Austen and then wonder why she's so popular. If your book veers too dramatically off course, your skim readers will come away with no idea what the book was about.
- Is your book too advanced for your audience, or too simplistic? Nobody likes to be patronised, but if your writing is too complex and you use too much of the jargon of your field when writing for the layman, even your skim readers will quit skimming and go watch Strictly Come Bake Off instead.
- Have you organised the information in your book in a logical order? Is it easy for the reader to follow? If it's not, if you jump about a bit, then now is the time to potentially reorder or restructure your book. It can be hellish work, but if it has to be done, it has to be done. Which is all the more reason to get it planned and plotted in advance, because even as a professional, even as a ghostwriter, restructuring makes me go, 'ugh'.
- Have you presented the information in a logical sequence?
- Have you scaffolded your chapter so that they build on one another meaningfully? Do they reflect the progression of your teachings accurately and comprehensively?
- Do your chapters transition from one another smoothly?
- Do you need to reorder any of your chapters to better highlight your information?

- Make sure you haven't used any ridiculously long sentences that might lose your reader halfway through. You're not Henry James, so don't do it. I remember occasionally causing the late great W.G. Sebald to complain about my odd, long sentences here and there. English wasn't his first language, and German is structured differently, and this meant he struggled at times when I went on too long. I quit doing it immediately. The man was up for a Nobel Prize. When someone like Sebald tells you to stop doing something, you stop doing it! RIP Max, you were utterly wonderful.
- Check over your paragraphs. Make sure each has a core topic and that you haven't overloaded them with too many changes of subject.
- If anything confuses you, get shot of it in a heartbeat. If anything confuses your mates when they read it, check their IQ is up to scratch, and then seriously think about changing it. Remember, a confused reader might start skimming, or worse, quit reading altogether.
- Check that all of your facts, figures, and references are reliable. If you're basing all your theories on someone who thinks the pyramids were built by aliens, you might want to reconsider (because everyone knows the moon was built by aliens, not the pyramids).
- Ensure you have any dates, statistics, and quotes correct. While you're at it, make sure you're not quoting someone who is morally tricky, as it brings your own name into question. And when I say this, I include any old quotes from Steve Jobs and Henry Ford. There are plenty of people out there who said amazing things who weren't abusive or racist. If you quote someone who's doing time for running a Ponzi scheme, I'm going to assume you're equally dodgy, so do steer

clear of bad people. If you're thinking about quoting Henry Kissinger, why not look and see if Frederick Douglass or Helen Keller said something you can use instead? And finally, always choose Jung over Freud, if possible.
- Make sure any names you've used are spelt correctly and that you've used any terminology properly.
- Have a last check of your sources and citations. Make sure they actually back up your claims. The most famously misused quote is 'The customer is always right.' Some dreadful businesses use it to make their staff deal with the outrageous and nonsensical demands their customers make. The correct quote is, in fact, 'The customer is always right in matters of taste.' Meaning, if your customers want everything in their lives to be beige, then you should probably stock a bunch of beige soft furnishings and keep your mouth shut on your own opinions of it.
- Finally, make sure all of your information is up-to-date. My reference to Tony Hart, which shall be coming up soon, doesn't count, cos he was brilliant.

USE OF AI IN EDITING

I work with a lot of people. Some write very well. Some aren't brilliant at writing but have phenomenal ideas. Some write fantastically in their first language, but having English as a second language restricts them somewhat. I adore the English language, but don't get me wrong, it's an absolute bugger sometimes. Just try teaching a foreign student phrasal verbs and you'll soon realise how flipping tricky it is. After all, the verb 'to have' is easy to understand. What's difficult is explaining why it means something completely different when you say, 'to have a go', 'to have it off', 'to have it out', 'to have at it', or, if you're Northern and you want to encourage someone, a simple 'HAVE IT!' will suffice.

I look back on my days teaching English and travelling fondly. I look back on trying to convince students that the verb 'to look' means something totally different when you say, 'look at', 'look after', 'look down on', 'look up to', and, 'look it over', with a feeling akin to exhaustion.

Right, let's get back to using AI to edit. Remember earlier when I said to make sure you stay on topic? Well, here was a good example of it going awry!

So, I've come across a heck of a lot of writers, both native and non-native English speakers, who write their book, then use AI to edit it. Morally, this is neither right nor wrong. It will, for example, get rid of all of those times you've incorrectly used 'myself' to sound posh. It will however, also try to whittle down your sentences to be as clear and as effective as possible.

And that's not always how good writing works.

Good writing gets the importance of pace. Good writing understands that some sentences need to be slowed down and some need to be punchy and direct. And AI, as it stands, doesn't comprehend this at all. It will simply suggest you make all of your sentences clean and direct.

So, you risk writing your entire book yourself, before using AI to go over it, only for it to turn out reading like something that has been entirely created by ChatGPT.

I have several clients who have come to me saying, 'I wrote it, then I got AI to fix it, but now can you make it human again?'

So what's my advice here?

Well, it's complicated. Let AI fix your errors and oftentimes, your punctuation too. But you don't have to accept all the changes it wants to make.

Take this gloriously hilarious opening sentence by Jane Austen:

'It is a truth universally acknowledged that a single man in possession of a good fortune, must be in want of a wife.'

If AI got its hands on this, it would change it to:

'A wealthy single man is always in search of a wife.'

It doesn't even mean the same thing anymore. The original sentence is one of the finest and funniest openings to a classic novel. Its pacing is spot on. Its roundabout way of speaking, highly suggests that it is not the single wealthy men that are of that opinion, but rather it comes from all of the hopeful young women and their families who want to marry into money. Add this to the fact that Jane Austen immediately quit the dating scene as soon as she got her first book published, and it's even more nuanced. However, by the time AI is finished with the sentence, it loses all of this suggestion, all of the humour, and all of its utterly wonderful pacing.

So, go ahead and use AI to fix your grammar and your punctuation; it'll help you with your semicolons beautifully. It'll also find little typos and errors that you might have missed. However, if it tries to dicker about with sentences, think twice before accepting the change. Your original sentences may be more nuanced, they may be paced better, they may be utterly wonderful. You don't want AI to muck it up and make it sound more direct and less human. What a huge shame it would be to write a book all on your own and then at the last minute turn it into AI slop.

Never forget:

Bad human writing is always, always preferable to AI writing.

Unless it's Twilight.

That's the exception.

You see, it's the person behind the work that makes it worth reading. And I know, I know, people are some of the worst creatures on the planet, but they're also some of the best. Remember Tony Hart? Wasn't he wonderful? (If you don't remember him, if you learnt how to type on a computer keyboard and not a manual typewriter, you'll have to take my word that Tony Hart was lovely. Also, you lot, I have great faith and hope in you. The kids are alright in my book; I think you're doing some wonderful things. Keep it up, I say. And also, sorry about this plastic-filled world you're inheriting. I did my best, but it's not really made a dent.)

Key Takeaways:

- Use AI in editing with caution
- Don't lose your voice, pace, meaning to AI's

- You risk it becoming a copyright or plagiarism concern if AI edits it too heavily
- Use to help identify issues with punctuation, grammar, and typos
- Be You!

TRADITIONAL PUBLISHING VS SELF-PUBLISHING VS HYBRI

This is the decision you're going to face when you've finished writing your book. How are you going to publish it? Do you want to try to get it published by a traditional publishing house? Are you going to have a bash at publishing it yourself? Or are you going to go down the hybrid route?

TRADITIONAL PUBLISHING
Let's talk about traditional publishing first. Traditional publishing is lovely if you can get it. A traditional publisher will get your book into the likes of Waterstones and WHSmith. You'll often get a lump sum of money upfront, with royalties if your book sells enough to cover that initial lump sum. Plus, your publisher will help a little with promotion. Although please note that they'll expect you to do the lion's share of promotion and will drop you like a Spudulike house special if you don't. In addition to this, if you're planning

on writing a second book and your first doesn't sell well, you'll be out of luck there too.

If you want to have a stab at traditional publishing, this is what you need to do:

Do not contact the publishing company directly. Manuscripts that are sent directly to a publishing house go straight onto the slushpile. A junior or an unpaid intern read through this slushpile and if a manuscript looks good, they'll hand it over to one of the publishing house editors. The Name of the Rose by Umberto Eco was found in a slushpile. You know, the one that was made into a film with Sean Connery, Christian Slater, and more excitingly, F Murray Abraham. F Murray Abraham! The man was in Blade Runner!

Getting published from the slushpile is very difficult. It's the acting equivalent of Hollywood producers discovering you as the next big star when you serve them a club sandwich in Denny's, or some other appropriately American-sounding dish and franchise.

Nowadays, not all publishing houses still bother to read the slushpile, so your chances of getting your book discovered are even slimmer. On top of this, it's a little bit disrespectful, because in these days of the interwebs, you can easily see from publishers' websites that they do not want you to send them unsolicited manuscripts (the exception to this is Mills & Boon, so fire away with your romance novels). So, if you want to be published via a traditional publishing house, you're going to need a literary agent.

How do you go about getting a literary agent?

Well, first of all, search for agents who deal with books in your field. If you send your book on toaster maintenance to a romance agent, you're not going to get far. Unless that is, you maintain toasters in a particularly steamy and smut-filled manner.

Once you have a list of agents who work within your field, check out who is open for new submissions, as well as who is new on the scene. Target them first. You'll have more chance with them. All agents let you know on their websites or listings how they want you to send your work to them. For example, most will only want the first 2,000 words or so, and they'll want it in a certain font and spacing etc. This sounds easy enough, but it's also a good idea to make your submission stand out. You'll have the chance to write a killer cover letter. Use it to tell them of your achievements and who you are. If you've won any awards, this will really help to get them interested, so if you don't have any, it's time to start entering a bunch of contests.

Get your social media and website up to scratch, as they'll be looking at how well you can publicise your book. This is important. I mean it. You could literally write the best book in your field, but you won't get an agent or publishing deal if they don't think you're marketable.

If you don't have an established name, if you're not second cousins to Peter Andre, it's not going to be easy. Publishing houses like to have some sort of guarantee that the book will sell. Having an audience already will only help your chances of getting a book deal.

If you manage to get a literary agent, and that agent gets you a book deal, then this is brilliant. Message me to let me know, because I'll be so happy for you. There is one thing to keep in mind, though: if you are trying to get your book done fast, ahead of your competition, it could take well over a year once you've had your book accepted, before it's published. So if you're racing to get your book out, traditional publishing might not be right for you. If you're not in a hurry, then it's wonderful. I am pre-emptively sipping champagne in celebration of you. Okay, it's not champagne, it's gin. And I'm gulping. But the sentiment is the same.

SELF-PUBLISHING

Self-publishing has gone through a bit of a revolutionary change over the years. It used to be considered a terrible idea, mainly because it was expensive and it meant a traditional publisher wouldn't touch you with whatever the modern equivalent of a ten-foot barge pole is.

Things have changed since then. It's cheaper now for a start. You won't end up with your back room filled with boxes of books that you can't shift, because you can sell your books directly through places like Amazon. Some excellent writers like Greg Dunnett started this way. His books are fantastic, and despite not getting a contract with a publishing company when he started writing, his books quite rightly gained so much attention when he self-published that he ended up being snapped up by a big one. There's also my dear friend's brother, who self-published a wonderful book of Christmas horror stories, where you read one a night like an advent calendar. It's great, especially the one where the mother replaces her family with scarecrows who have better manners.

The main issue surrounding self-publishing, and particularly when you're using your book to promote your business, is that you have to get it right. Doing it on your own is totally fine, but if your writing is a bit dodgy, if it's full of mistakes, it's not going to reflect well on your business. This also goes for the state of your published book. If it's formatted amateurishly, it's going to look rubbish, which in turn will make you look bad. So, my advice for self-publishing is go for it, but only if you know what you're doing. Because if you screw it up, it'll do more harm than good to your reputation.

HYBRID-PUBLISHING

Hybrid publishing can be, for many, the Goldilocks porridge that's just right. You get professional editing, design, and formatting, and you get the book you want. A good hybrid publisher won't publish any old tosh; they'll make sure your book is up to standard, because it will reflect on them just as much as it reflects on you. You'll get a polished, perfected product out of it.

With hybrid publishing you've got professionals in your corner. You're not alone. Here at Writing Dr, we can help you every step of the way, and we'll get you a readable, professional-looking book out for when you need it.

You're the expert in your field; we're the experts in making sure your books show it.

Key Takeaways:

- Lump sum and smaller royalties with Traditional Publishing
- Traditional publishers will help with promotion, but you're expected to do a lot yourself
- Require a literary agent to get into a traditional publisher
- Write your best-ever cover letter
- Ensure your social media, traditional media, and website are all first class, they'll be checking to see if you can self-promote
- Have a large audience who are wanting your book
- Self-publishing is much more common now
- Amazon and others, will publish your book on demand, so you don't need two rooms of your house full of books
- Ensure you get it right, you want your book to enhance your reputation. Do not risk damaging your reputation with a badly edited/formatted book
- Use a reputable hybrid-publisher...like Writing Dr
- Writing Dr will ensure that your book is perfectly written, edited, formatted, and will help you get it published in a variety of formats
-

HOW TO USE YOUR BOOK FOR LEADS

The best reason an entrepreneur or coach has for writing a book is to generate leads. Use your book to showcase your business, and make sure to tell them where they can find you to work with you. So many books today even include QR codes, as mentioned earlier, to bring the readers to their websites. It's worth saying again that it can be a great idea to have links to pictures or further information on your website. You can also get people into your CRM this way. You can even promise an extra chapter of your book to people who pop their email address into your website. Think also about the possibility of creating workbooks or checklists to accompany your book on your website. Make it a little interactive!

Many extremely successful entrepreneurs give their book away free in exchange for an email address. It's an amazing way to win potential customers over. Take this book for example. This is my opportunity to demonstrate that I know what I'm talking about and that I'm approachable. I'm often told to keep my doctorate secret because some people will a) find it intimidating, or b) think I want to write everything in a bombastic, overly academic way.

Can I write in a bombastic, overly academic way?

Of course I can!

Do I think this style will interest anyone who isn't a hardcore professor of literature?

Hell no!

I'm not even sure it interests literature professors, to be honest.

So, this book is important as a lead generator for me, too. It tells you what sort of knowledge and expertise I have, and it helps let you know what sort of decent old bean I am.

This has also been mentioned previously, but it's worth repeating, you can use your books to secure yourself speaking gigs, podcasts, talks, workshops, webinars, all of the things! Once people know you've got enough material on your field of expertise to give a talk, they'll start wanting you to come and speak to them. And your book will place you head and shoulders, and perhaps elbows and stomach, above your competition.

It is said that Amazon is one of the web's biggest search engines. So get on it! With a book, you'll find yourself reaching so many more people.

What else?

You can use your book to show off case studies, or direct people to your website to see them. Absolutely use it instead of a business card. Think of it as a kind of passive networking. You might be in your bathroom freezing off a verruca, but your ideal customers could be reading your book and thinking about working with you.

Don't worry, I'm sure they have verrucas too.

Normally, networking means you meet someone, you shake hands, and you hand each other business cards that end up getting lost. If you're really slick, you cut to the chase and connect via LinkedIn or whatever your professional social media of choice is. But then, you sort of forget about each other. However, if you hand your book over, BAM, you're unforgettable, and you'll be the first person they think of when they or their acquaintances need your services.

Seriously.

You'll be as unforgettable as Nemo's performance at the 2025 Eurovision Song Contest. And that wasn't just unforgettable, that was art.

Key Takeaways:

- Offer your book for free, link them into your CRM
- Get onto Amazon and other book stores
- Drive customers to your website, buy your products/services, or to book a call with you
- Open doors with media and podcast opportunities
- Your best business card

See you soon, writingdr.com/book-a-call

SELLING IT, PRICING IT, GIVING IT AWAY

With hybrid publishing, your books are most valuable as a way to market yourself, to advertise your business, to connect to people, to steer people towards your services, and to consolidate your personal brand. It's not really a way to make millions from book sales alone.

It's a good idea to keep this in mind when selling it, pricing it, or, as the title suggests, giving it away.

If you decide to sell your book, remember you don't just have to sell your book on Amazon. You can sell it on your own website, or you can sell it after doing talks or conferences. If you often have a table at networking events, you can pile it high with your books and sell them there, too.

How to price it, though?

If you use a hybrid publishing company, they'll give you an idea of how you should price your book, but ultimately, the decision comes down to you. As with everything, I think research is key. Take a look at how other books in your field are priced and use this as a guideline. What you're probably going to find is that most business books are sold between £7.99 and £14.99. So, somewhere in this range, depending on your subject matter and the length of your book, is probably about right. Occasionally, I really want to read a non-fiction book which is priced around £150.00, and in those circumstances, I just get my local library to get it in, and so might your ideal clients.

While thinking about your pricing, you're going to have to make a decision on how to price the hardback, paperback, and eBook versions. You may want to put a discount on whichever you want people to buy the most of. If you reduce your paperback for example, it could help you sell enough to raise your ranking on Amazon for paperback books in your field. Generally, however, eBooks are the cheapest option, and that, coupled with how fast your readers can get their mitts on your book, is often the version people will buy the most on a whim. So, many authors keep eBook pricing low.

How low?

Well, that's another debate you're going to have to have. If it's not low enough, will people buy it? If it's too low, will people lose respect for it?

One way to get around this conundrum is to price it reasonably, then offer discounts from time to time that coordinate with publicity events, such as during talks or podcasts, or even as a special launch price for the first couple of days your book goes on sale. This way, your customer will have more of an increased perception of the value of your book.

So, now onto the third option. Giving your book away. Giving your book away might feel like a terrifying prospect. You might think that all your hard work deserves some sort of compensation, and it does. Of course it does! But giving it away has some perks worth considering.

You can distribute your books to potential clients liberally. Nobody likes to buy an expensive product or a decently priced service on first hearing about a company or meeting you. Your potential clients may not have even considered your services before meeting you, so it's going to take them a little time to digest how much better you can make their lives. Studies show that before people buy a service, they need to have encountered you or your company seven times, either face-to-face or online or via advertising. If, on one of those encounters, you hand them your book, you will seriously improve your chances of selling to them. Because rather than having to wait and hope they see one of your posts or advertisements, you've got their attention, page after page of it (if you write well). They'll come to know you, hopefully, if you've done it right, they'll start to like you and trust in your ability. And before they finish your book, they'll prefer to work with you rather than some company they've seen advertised on Facebook in between the lost dog posts and the wine mummy videos. No disrespect to mothers who enjoy a decent Beaujolais, or people with exuberant dogs with no sense of direction. I've never had a dog, but I have had a small flock of utterly wonderful ducks who were expert escapologists, and it's terribly embarrassing when one sneaks into a neighbour's garden and you have to go round and ask if you can have your duck back, please.

So, giving your book away free.

It sounds counterproductive, but it's worth contemplating. If it helps you secure clients, you might find it's worth it. Certainly, entrepreneurs have found enormous success this way, so it's a tried and tested technique that works.

Here at Writing Dr, you may have noticed we do a bit of a mixture. At speaking events, we hand out our books for free. In fact, you might be reading this because I have personally handed it to you with my own delicate and graceful hands. You might be reading this because you downloaded it free of charge during a special offer while we were doing a workshop. If that's the case, hello! How lovely to see you again! You've probably already spotted how very much more eloquent I am on paper than when I'm opening my gob in front of a room full of people. I apologise, it's what happens when you've spent your education and career alone in a room with a pen and paper. I do hope I made sense, if I didn't, go ahead and ask me questions, but do speak up, my hearing is shot.

So, there you have it. The most important thing is you get your book into the hands of your clients. It's up to you how you want to go about it. And if you're thinking of getting ducks, I'm happy to answer any questions on that, too. Bloody wonderful little weirdos they are, I enjoyed every second of owning them.

BOOK DESCRIPTIONS AND KEY WORDS

Once your book is on sale online, you're going to find out that you can make or break it in terms of sales, depending on how well you utilise your book description and keywords.

I almost don't want to write this chapter, because it's going to take the art form that is writing and reduce it to random words that will be most likely picked up in searches.

Ugh.

But it's got to be done, and it's got to be done well.

Personally, when I read the descriptions of a book to see if I want to read it or not, I'm not looking at how many key search words they use. I'm looking at how interesting or relevant the book is to what I want. However, if you're searching for a book online, the internet won't find it for you if the author and publisher haven't used the keywords you've used in your search in their description. So in a way, you're writing your book description and keywords for search engines just as much, if not more, than you're writing them for a human potential reader.

Now is not the time to be artistic, I'm afraid. Now is the time to think like a computer. What words might people who want to read your book type into the search bar? And what words do the search engines need to see to bring your book up?

Sometimes it takes a computer to know how a computer thinks, so feel free at this point to ask AI to help you come up with a list of keywords.

Use your SEO words from your website too, as there's a good chance you already have a library of keywords at your disposal. Put them to use when you publish your book. Use as many variations as you can think of, it'll all help to get your book noticed by whichever search engine your potential clients are using.

CONCLUSION

Well, dear reader, thank you for getting all the way to the end with us. I do hope we've given you a damn good idea of how to write your book, while demonstrating the techniques as we went along.

Writing is an art form, yes, but art can always be learnt. After all, I taught myself how to cross-stitch celebrity portraits. You should see my Sean Bean. It's a masterpiece.

If there are two things that I would really like you to come away from this book knowing, it's that you must inform and entertain. If you nail those two things, you'll make your audience happy. I don't care if you entertain them by being funny, dramatic, or tragic; just keep them reading.

And so I shall leave you with my own version of:
   Morituri te salutant
(Those who are about to die salute you)
Which is this:
Qui scribent, te salutant
(Those who are about to write, I salute you)
Now stop reading, pick up a pen, and git 'er done.

ABOUT THE AUTHOR

If you've read the book, you likely feel like you know us already, but if you are starting here... then go to the beginning and start reading and follow our process and get your business book written!

If you're flicking through this book in a library, then go to the lovely librarian with the book, or the machine and book it out. If you're in a shop, buy it.

Then write your best business book with the tips, tricks, and techniques within it.

If you've read the book and are looking to know more about us, then...

Dr Nicola Russell Johnson

Dr Nicola Russell Johnson loves to help people realise their dream of having a book. She has a PhD in Creative Writing and over 15 years of experience helping people write. The number of topics she's written about are more numerous than Justin Bieber's number one singles. She was going to insert a joke here using some lyrics from one of his songs, but suddenly realised she doesn't know any.

Nicola believes everyone has a book in them, and it's her job to make the task of writing seem less daunting.

She's a master at utilising different styles and techniques, prides herself on her ability to entertain, and has impeccable handwriting.

She's always buzzing with ideas, always has a notebook about her person, and always has dishes in the sink.

She'll get round to them later. Right now she's on a writing streak.

Peter Russell

Often seven cups of tea in by lunchtime, Peter Russell has racked up skills like Ronnie O'Sullivan racks up balls. He used to be a detective in the CID, plus he's an accredited life coach, coaching in the public and private sector. He's also a writer in his own right, having helped create a course and exam for pilots and air traffic controllers. Finally, he's lived and taught English all round the world and has the flawless grammar to prove it.

When he's not interviewing clients and publishing books, he's running a football team for children with disabilities, volunteering as the welfare officer for their club and the safeguarding strategy lead for Cheshire FA and functioning as a governor for a nearby special needs school. All of this is probably the reason for the seven cups of tea before lunch.

He loves to help people, and this is what he'll do for you, work with you until your book is published, making sure you're on track, holding you to account, and pulling you through it. Your clients deserve to hear your story, and you deserve the help to get you there.

CONNECT WITH US

Linked In
www.linkedin.com/in/peter-russell-writing-coach-and-publisher-280149208/
www.linkedin.com/in/dr-nicola-russell-johnson-711619350/
Facebook
www.facebook.com/peter.russell.927
www.facebook.com/nicola.russelljohnson
Tik Tok
www.tiktok.com/@writingdr.com
Instagram
www.instagram.com/writingdrs/
You Tube
www.youtube.com/@Writing_Dr

www.ingramcontent.com/pod-product-compliance
Lightning Source LLC
Chambersburg PA
CBHW052034070526
44584CB00016B/2034